Navakarma

Navakarma

Nine Philosophies for Curing Diseases
Like Hormonal Imbalance, Anxiety, and
Depression, Using Natural Remedies

Shreya Nath

PARTRIDGE

To order additional copies of this book, contact
Partridge India
000 800 10062 62
orders.india@partridgepublishing.com

www.partridgepublishing.com/india

Contents

Disclaimer

Reasonable care has been taken to ensure that the information presented in this book is accurate. All treatments suggested will not produce side effects, but exceptions can happen, so the treatment has to be taken at the reader's sole discretion. Also the reader should understand that the information provided does not constitute legal, medical, or professional advice of any kind.

Indebted to life, force, air, wind, spirit, breath, *ruh*, energy, light, God, nature, Indian ancient scriptures, parents, and family.

Dedicated to all readers because this experiential learning and sharing is for them.

'Ms Shreya used to get sonography done at my clinic, and most of the time, the diagnosis was bulky uterus and thickened endometrium. The last scan taken on 9/4/13 showed normal uterus and no abnormality. I was happy to learn from her that she was taking precautions and has become healthy. She should share this experience with as many people as possible' (Dr Rajeev Nagi, MD (radio diagnosis), proprietor of Nagi Imaging X-Ray and Ultrasound Clinic, Nagpur, India).

'Shreya came to my clinic for menorrhagia and related symptoms. She responded well to the treatment as she was regular. I am happy to know that she overcame the disease without surgery' (Dr Veena Deo, MD, BAMS, Ayurvedic practitioner, *nadi tadnya* (Reg. No. I-16535)).

'Shreya was my patient for minerics therapy for eighteen months for menopausal syndrome (endometriosis and bulky uterus). She responded very well to this therapy. She was very regular and gave the needed information at the right time; hence, results were positive' (Dr Farwah Husain, DHMS Reg. (No. 14781), Healix Medical Centre).

'We are delighted to learn that Shreya could benefit from *panchakarma* treatment. I strongly believe that her positive attitude and smiling nature had a big role to play in the recovery process. We take pride in our customised detoxification programme and top quality herbs. Testimonials from valued guests like her give us confidence to evolve, improve in order to benefit society at large' (Ms Shruti Singhal, CEO of Baidyanath Life Sciences).

Acknowledgements

Navakarma for Holistic Healing

While the story is mine, the journey was successful because of contributions from various people, systems, beliefs, which provided insight at different stages. The book is based on my healing experience using natural remedies with a scientific approach. The chapter 'Thirty-Six Months to a Healthy Uterus' documents the events and marks the role of the womb for the specific period of nine months in every woman's life. It also signifies the patience required for thirty-six-months healing tenure. The healing might have started earlier, but it showed the positive results (normal uterus and endometrium) only after thirty-six months. I am writing this book in 2016, and I can assure you that healing is complete.

The advice from doctors of all streams (allopathy, Ayurvedic, homeopathy) and my parents, husband, sister, brother, sister-in-laws, and supportive children, Nishchay and Stuti, made this happen. My children and husband especially contributed in the making of this book by providing needed help in mudra pictures, diagrams, flow charts, book title, etc.

Spiritual master Dr Balaji Tambe's CDs *Yoga Nidra* I and II were my guardian angels since 1995. He is my sound guru because, by listening to these particular CDs, I was able to experience light in my heart chakra in May 2005, and I listened to these CDs for at least 200 days out of the 365 days without fail since 2005. They were instrumental in strengthening my meditation journey. I am indebted and deeply grateful for the experience I have gained from his healing music.

My father, Kamal Narayan Seetha, brought a wealth of experience in our life. He is an accomplished person in the field of yoga, *rudraksha* (a spiritual bead from India), and chakra meditation using sound and colour therapy. He has authored *The Power of Rudraksha*, a bestseller in the segment. He is a gifted therapist and a perpetual researcher in the fields of chakra meditation and healthy living.

A guided chakra meditation CD named *Santulan* is an amazing creation by him along with Indian musicians. In this CD, the ancient *beej* mantra (sound) and colour (light) associated with each sound and the location of energy centres is explained and sung according to each chakra in such a way that they energise the chakras. This composition takes you to a level where you experience self-realisation.

Cover Page:
The Apple Artwork *Eternal Identity*

It is so aptly said that when you want something, the universe transpires to make it happen for you. I reside just 2 kilometres away from Sachee Art Gallery, which is located in an area called Sadar (Nagpur, India), and for all the two decades of my stay in Nagpur, I never stepped into it although I passed by it several times.

When the decision to finally make the book happen had taken place in my mind, I told my daughter one day, 'Let's check out some artefacts for home decoration or gift purposes at Sachee.' This was where this painting caught my attention. The artist had drawn a correlation between an apple and the womb. I was always emotional about the womb being the nurturer of life, and the removal of the womb being suggested was shaking my consciousness.

On my enquiry about it at the art gallery, the gracious owner connected me to the artist.

The apple might have been the forbidden fruit, but that didn't stop artist Wahida Ahmed from making it her muse.

'Have you noticed an apple?' she asked. 'For me, it resembles the womb of a woman, where the origin of life takes place, and that's where my interest in painting apples began.'

I asked her about the beehive-like structure on the apple, and she said, 'Bees are like humans, especially women. They work hard not just for themselves but for the entire family.'

The cover page work shows an apple having an old tree growing out of it and with birds returning to it.

'The tree represents older women, like our grandmothers or mothers. Even when they become old, just like the tree, they offer the same protection and love,' she says.

Thank you, Wahida, for sharing this profound work of art called *Eternal Identity*. For me, the womb, beehive, and apple also signify the nectar of life for the unborn—truly the start of life.

The images of Surya namaskar were provided by Janardan Swami Yogabhyasi Mandal, Ramnagar, Nagpur (India). You can also visit www.jsyog.org to see videos of yoga practices.

The energy centre diagram has been made by the advertising agency www.sachinnovations.com.

I am equally thankful to the great Internet, Google, and the innumerable health and medical websites and bulletins that educated me on this path.

The book is self-written, and it might have language flaws. I have tried to share the maximum, and there can be some suggestions that might not agree with you, which you can leave, but still there can be some takeaways that you will cherish.

Being a first time author I was ably supported by Pohar Baruah, Amanda Dayham, Kim Lacey and many more team members of patridge publishing. I am thankful for their professional advice.

Navakarma

(*Nava* Means 'Nine', and *Karma* means 'Results for Your Actions') Philosophy

If you want to be healthy then stop being unhealthy!

It is easy to say it, but once you start applying it, there is so much happiness because you have control over your life. These navakarmas have emerged from the desire to have more control over the mind, body, and spirit even when in this fast-paced, materialistic world there is dissatisfaction of all sorts, which has created imbalance.

Look around you, and you will find two extremes in our society. The first extreme is, there is a handful of people who have unlimited creativity, wealth, health, knowledge, new inventions, new goals, positive relationships, and strength of mind. These same people in their past lives were in the other extreme and had pulled themselves out. On the other hand, there is a large chunk of society which is riddled with despair, depression, anxiety, low self-esteem, poverty, disease, suicidal tendencies, drugs, etc. There are rich people who have sufficient wealth but suffer from low self-esteem, poor health, and negative relationships. So materialism also needs balance just as poverty needs it.

A complete person operates from the centre of his being. Even this person has to operate in a world which has hate, terrorism, war, pollution, adulteration of food, diseases, etc. How does one keep the balance? These navakarmas, or nine actions, when practised with complete awareness, can unlock the cause-and-effect theory and unleash your full potential.

1. knowledge or gyan for mental balance
2. food or khaan for nutritional balance
3. water or *pan* for water balance
4. allopathy, Ayurveda, homeopathy, minerics therapy for health balance
5. exercise/yoga for body balance
6. meditation or dhyana for spiritual balance
7. work or *kaam* for social balance
8. charity or *daan* for emotional balance
9. application and assimilation of advice or *saam* for holistic balance

We are living in a world where the human race is getting challenged by its own excesses (such as air, water, and sound pollution; increased consumption of processed foods and genetically modified foods, mind and lifestyle pollution, overdependence on allopathic drugs). Also we all know what is harming us, but still we do not want to exercise our willpower to remove any of these excesses that are eroding us. The *effect* of an ailment finds more focus in our lives than the *causes*. Medical help and drugs are necessary for overcoming them, and if the medical therapists can make us aware of the side effects and prescribe precautions to overcome post-recovery problems, it can lessen the side effects, and also there is compassion in this transaction.

The need to strike a balance is my purpose in writing this book because after healing myself completely from a potentially disastrous health trauma, I felt that anyone who is in a similar situation can benefit from my experience. The navakarma philosophy came into being after the churning process of handling diseases in my daily life and tasting the nectar of a disease-free life without medicines, which resulted in my penning this book. Achieving mental, nutritional, water, health, body, spiritual, social, emotional, and holistic balance is all that is navakarma. Also an open mind and willpower will be required to get the benefits from the suggested remedies.

I was diagnosed with bulky uterus, and it took thirty-six months of navakarma before I was able to achieve a healthy uterus! It was a holistic healing of a uterus of twelve weeks size which had a 23 -millimetre endometrium. This true story gives proven tips to overcome *hormonal imbalance* in a *natural way*. You can see the application and assimilation of all philosophies, approaches, elements, and advice being implemented practically. This can be used for any kind of suffering or malady which has roots in mental or emotional plane. It cannot be recommended for emergency situations, like a fever, injury, heart attack.

Thirty-Six Months to
a Healthy Uterus:
A True Story of Natural Healing

The year 2009 was coming to an end, and I was busy as ever with the demands of my organisation, Headstart, an executive-search firm. I was feeling wonderful as the year went by smoothly as per my expectation. In the new year, my father was organising a workshop on chakra meditation. I extended my help in conducting it, and it was a success. January passed by, and that was when I noticed an abnormality in my menstrual cycle. My period dates came at around the fifth of each month. I was in a state of utter confusion and more so because my cycles had been perfect like a clock and I was not feeling any other symptoms.

It was in May 2009 that I went for a complete health check-up, including a pap test (refer to ANX 1 for the sonography report and ANX 2 for the PAP test).

SONOGRAPHY OF ABDOMEN AND PELVIS

Liver is normal in size shape and echotexture. No evidence of focal intra hepatic space occupying lesion. IHBR are not dilated .

CBD and portal vein appears normal in caliber.

Gall bladder is normal in size and does not contain echogenic densities causing distal acoustic shadowing.

Pancreas normal in shape and echotexture. No evidence of para aortic lymphadenopathy

Spleen normal in size and echo pattern.

Both kidneys normal in size, shape, contour and echotexture. Cortical thickness and echogenicity appears normal .
Right kidney measures - 9.7 X 3.9 cm
Left kidney measures – 9.2 X 4.3 cm

Absence of calculus focal mass or changes of hydronephrosis.
CMD maintained.

No evidence of free fluid in abdomen.

Bladder well distended appears clear.

Ureters not dilated.

Uterus normal in size. Central uterine cavity echoes appear normal. Ovaries delineated on either side and appear normal. No evidence of abnormal adnexal mass lesion

No free fluid in pouch of Douglas .

OPINION : NO DEMONSTRABLE ABNORMALITY IN ABDOMEN AND PELVIS.

ANX 1

Name : Mrs.Sherya Nath   Age / Sex : 41yrs / Female

Date : May 8, 2009

CYTOLOGY REPORTS

SPECIMEN   :-   Cervical Scrape Smear

SLIDE NO   :-   CH/ CY/ 155/ 09

MICROSCOPY:- Smears is satisfactory for evaluation limited by absence of
endocervical cells Smears show predominantly intermediate with superficial
squamous cells against mild inflammatory background..

IMPRESSION:-   Smear within normal limit.

INTERPRETATION :-   Negative for intraepithelial lesion or neoplasia

NOTE   :-   2 slides enclosed

ANX 1

I decided to wait till the 5 February 2010, but there was no sign of my period again. That was when I immediately made an appointment with Dr Gayatri, a renowned gynaecologist at a leading hospital at Nagpur. On 7 February, she examined and suggested medicines and the pregnancy test to rule out the first possibility of the missing-period symptom. At forty-three years with two children at seventeen and fifteen years of age, I cannot grin at this news. So for the first time in my life, I bought the pregnancy test kit, which I used to notice in the ads and only imagined would be used by teenagers who got entangled in unwanted pregnancies. To my great relief, the test was negative.

On 7 February 2010, suddenly my menstruation began, and I was again thanking my stars that the ordeal was over. It actually was going to last till 2013, but at that very moment I, never knew what was in store. The period went on for the next two weeks, and I was again in panic. I consulted with my elderly full-time maidservant, whom we fondly called Amma, and we drew the logical conclusion that since I had missed the last period in December, I might be getting the double doze. Anyway, on 24 February, I contacted Dr Gayatri again for a check-up. An ultrasonography (USG) was done, which showed a normal uterus with an endometrial thickness of 13 millimetres and a cyst of 18 millimetres on the right ovary (see ANX 3). She told me it could be a case of hormonal imbalance, and she prescribed medicines. Also she told me that such bleeding was abnormal, so to rule out cancer, I must also get a D & C done. (Diagnostic surgery is explained in the chapter on the fourth navakarma, allopathy section.)

Patient data		Exam data	
Name	MRS. SHREYA NATH	Request date	24/02/10
Age / sex	42 Y / F	Exam date / Time	24/02/10 AT 1:01 PM
	OPD	Referring physician	

ULTRASONOGRAPHY OF PELVIS

Clinical information: []

Comparisons: [Not available]

Real time B mode gray scale ultrasound examination of pelvis shows,

Urinary bladder is well filled with smooth and regular outline with normal wall (4 mm) thickness.
Uterus is normal in size .The echotexture of uterus is normal, no evidence of solid or cystic lesion seen. Endometrial thickness is 13 mm. Both the ovaries are normal in size , right ovary shows one follicular cyst (18 mm). There is no solid or cystic mass lesion seen in either adnexa.
No free fluid seen in cul-de-sac.
Right iliac fossa show no abnormality.

INTERPRETATION:
1. No significant abnormality detected in pelvis.
2. Endometrial thickness 13 mm.

Recommendation: [Nil]

Report date / time   February 24, 2010 at 1:25 pm

ANX 3

She decided to stabilise me through medication and then suggested that I get a D & C. I believe most of the patients have a great sense of relief after meeting a doctor, especially an allopathic one because the cure of all maladies is instant and it puts you back on your feet soon. It was the first time that I had heard these terminologies—'Endometrial thickness is 13 millimetres', 'D & C', etc.—and I was told that I would be bleeding for a couple of days more as the *endometrium lining* had not shed. Due to lack of physical activities and prolonged bleeding, I was also gaining some weight and was always in a stressful and exhausted mood.

I have been an entrepreneur and career-oriented person, so multitasking was always second nature to my personality. But here I had to balance my illness, juggling with the day-to-day challenges of running an organisation in a volatile market while holding the fort for my teenage children (Nishchay and Stuti in their eleventh and ninth standard respectively) when so many turning-point decisions had to be made. Our son Nishchay was in the merit list in his Xth standard and was preparing for competitive exams in engineering, like for IIT. The silver lining has always been my caring husband, for whom family is the final destination, so he can definitely give some valuable tips on how he made himself a great pillar by juggling work, home, and sleepless nights.

The medicines did not work, so I was told to start with hormone replacement therapy (HRT). I remembered that there were articles that I had read somewhere on its negative effects. But then, for most of the allopathic medicines that you pop, there are always some bad effects (somehow the cure part is what we appreciate, so we do not want to glance at the side effects). I started with the HRT. My husband, Sanjay, also sometimes joined me in doing Google search on the symptoms that I was having (i.e. hormonal imbalance, menorrhagia, endometrial thickness). The search did give many meanings to all these complicated biological phenomena but did not give very positive feelings as most of the searches always led to the possibility of cancer. Everything—from the thickness of the endometrium to unexplained bleeding and to a bulky uterus—pointed to the dreadfully sounding word *cancer*.

Day in, day out, I was becoming stressed and obsessed with the cancer threat lurking round the corner. I had never been so interested in knowing the gynaecological side of my female friends and relatives so much as I was then. I was curious to know the types of problems they had faced or were undergoing. I realised to my utter dismay that most of them had hysterectomies done, and they were bravely claiming that it was a simple surgery and they were back to their routine. There was one close relative who had a similar diagnosis like mine, and she said that she was managing her bulky uterus for the last ten years. Ten years! It did not sound motivating enough, but she was fit and healthy and had not done away with her uterus, so that definitely gave me some flicker of hope. I also came across two family friends who were gynaecologists and had hysterectomies done. So it was not an uncommon thing to get this surgery done as even medical practitioners were sure about this treatment for menstrual disorders.

Panic attacks, night sweats, feelings of sorrow and hollowness were slowly engulfing me. I was blaming myself for not exercising enough, sitting in the office chair for a prolonged time, having tea and coffee, snacking on chocolates, chips, samosas (Indian fried puffs filled with spiced potatoes), etc. Every small sinful delight that I had indulged merrily in the past now looked like monsters that had struck my body. I started feeling more receptive to newspaper and TV news mentioning facts and figures on how many suffer from various cancers, especially in the reproductive system. All this added to my woes. I had also lost my sister-in-law to uterine cancer and had a couple of relatives fighting breast cancer and ovary tumours and cancer. So all the conversations, memories, images, and news from friends, relatives, and unknown people succumbing to cancer started overwhelming me.

I had least bothered about the location of various organs in my body—like the uterus, ovaries, cervix—and what their functions were. I had vaguely heard about oestrogen and progesterone but never bothered because all these years, they had not bothered me anyway. But now I was seeking information on them tirelessly.

The periods were always there—some days less and some days heavy. But they never left my body. I was supplementing my body with iron and calcium tablets and also eating a well-balanced diet, but the anxiety and prolonged bleeding plunged me into despair. I was also scared of the side effects of HRT. In today's data-filled world, we have so much information being doled out on cancer that every situation in the form of lump, bleeding, weakness, etc. is perceived immediately as a cancer threat. Cancer is spreading, but there is so much hype around it that there are other deadly diseases—like meningitis, TB, viruses, or even diabetes—which don't get that much amount of permanent focus as cancer gets.

The entire February, I was having bleeding episodes. The clots were bigger, and my iron count dipped from fourteen to eleven. I decided to disclose this to my parents, brother, and sister, who resided in Mumbai. They immediately swung into action and introduced me to Dr Leena, a renowned consultant in gynaecology and obstetrics at one of India's best multi-speciality hospital located at Mumbai. I sent her my reports online, and she also advised HRT and then D & C.

For a week, I had her prescription. Then somehow my inner voice started questioning the sequence of events in my life. All along I had never had menstrual problems, so could it be an early menopause? My mother had it in her late fifties, but after speaking to her, I came to know that my aunts from the maternal side had early menopause and one of them had to be hospitalised for menorrhagia. But still my situation was getting out of control.

My husband is a well-read astrologer. I am a non-believer in rituals and astrology, but the situation had overpowered all my belief systems and I consulted him about my *kundali* (birth chart). He said it showed minor surgery but ruled out the deadly cancer disease. I tried to believe him completely, but doubt was more supreme. We also did a Mahamritunjay Jaap (a recitation of mantra for longevity) and havan (also known as yajna or *homa*, a sacred purifying ritual done in front of the fire, using grains, ghee or butter, and herbs to remove negative effects).

By March, and I was still bleeding heavily, and I was changing pads almost every hour or two. The bleeding would recede only when I took medicines, so I decided to catch the next flight to Mumbai and succumb myself to the best practices of medical fraternity. I had done some googling on D & C and felt that this would be an important diagnosis to decide my next course of action, about which I was completely fuzzy at that moment. Dr Leena fixed 25 March as the date for the D & C and hysteroscopy.

On the evening of 23 March, I was at my parents' place at Mumbai. My worried mother had her kitchen and fridge loaded with fruits, sprouts, coconut water, and all types of nutritive food to strengthen me. In India, parents show maximum attention through food. We are from Rajasthan State in India, and food is the succour for all maladies. Every disease is cured through food. There are natural remedies for everything. Even if your stomach is full, there is something to eat to help in digesting what is inside.

Since February, I had switched over to dark-coloured clothes, and my multiple handbags always had sanitary napkins in it. During that period, I was in a different time zone and had forgotten about how a day could be without anxiety. I had been in and out of menorrhagia for almost sixty days by then. I had a restless night, and my mother was getting up every time I twisted and turned and, even in the middle of night, was offering all the nutritious food that she had stacked. Early morning just before sunrise, my father called me to be with him at the balcony, and he wanted to show some yogic postures and pranayama (read Chapter 5 for more details) that would be beneficial. He also had earlier told me about the benefits of viewing the sun just for a few minutes during sunrise.

As usual, we love to know about beneficial things, but when it comes to practice, we postpone it for another day, which only happens when we are in trouble. As it was just impossible for me to exercise, I welcomed the sun god by staring at the rising sun for a minute or two. The moment I closed my eyes, I saw an impression of the Om symbol in between the eyebrows—*agya* chakra (see the chapter on the sixth navakarma, for meditation). This amazed me, and I tried to reason it out as an illusion. Despite having a scientific bent of mind, sometimes the "Doubting Thomas" takes over. So when miracles happen, it exhilarates me for that particular moment; then after some time, my reasoning cap takes over.

I skipped breakfast because I was not sure whether the tests needed an empty stomach. In all my nervousness and excitement, I had not asked for the kind of tests I would be undergoing before the D & C. On 24 March, Dr Leena examined the ultrasonography scan that I was carrying from Nagpur (ANX 4 shows USG of pelvis, stating enlarged uterus and 23-millimetre endometrium). I underwent all the prescribed tests that were mandatory before surgery on the same day.

Name of Patient :Mrs   Shreya Nath

Reference By   Self

Dated   : 23-3--10.

SONOGRAPHY OF PELVIS .

The urinarybladder is moderately distended and normal
No intraluminal mass or calculus is seen
Uterus is enlarged and bulky (106x61x53mm) with coarse myometrium
N o evidence of focal mass / fibroid or gestational sac
Endometrium is   23 mm thick/regular
Cervix is normal.

Rt ovary measures-28x17mm .
Lt ovary measures 26x20mm
Both ovaries are normal in size/location

Parametria are clear.

No free-fluid seen in cul-de-sac.

Both the iliac regions are clear

OPINION: Enlarged and bulky uterus showing grossly thick endometrium with coarse myoetrium..? adenomyosis

Anex 4

The next day, on 25 March, I had to report for the D &
C test. At home, I could see that everyone was trying to
be in a happy-go-lucky mood, but I knew all were anxious
about the outcome of the next day's surgery. We'd always
anticipated the worst, and this was a universal phenomenon.
Again I was twisting and turning, and my mother ensured
that I had all the nutritive food before 10 p.m. because after
that, I was not supposed to eat due to surgery. Thanks to
our great mothers, who overfeed us and help us stock all
that love and nutrition in the form of fat for such rainy
days in our lives. Out of inquisitiveness, I again checked
out the morning sun, and this time, I was thrilled to see the
Om symbol again. I thanked God for being with me, and
suddenly, I felt positive about the day.

The hospital was remarkably neat, clean, well organised,
and tastefully done. Everything was meticulously lined
up, and I was wheeled into the ICU (intensive-care unit)
for surgery. I was bleeding and changing pads and before
going into the ICU, I also went and changed a pad.
While lying down in the OT (operation theatre) when
I was waiting for my turn for the surgery, I felt a great
sensation of calmness in my mind and body. I was in
a meditative state. I have been a regular practitioner of
dhyana or meditation since 2005 (see the chapter on the
sixth navakarma), and I was saying silent prayers for all
that was happening.

The surgery procedure followed, and when I was coming
out of the effect of the anaesthesia, I started shivering and
indicated this to the attendant. The nurse helped out by
putting under my sheet a pipe with warm air gushing out.

After a couple of hours, I had stabilised and was discharged in the early evening. The after-effects of this surgery are almost nil. In fact, I went along with my brother to his office just after being discharged. In the evening, we all had great family time, but at the back in all our minds was the outcome of the D & C report that we were going to get the next day.

The wait for the D & C reports that were going to be given next day looked eternal. In all my waking hours, I was feeling shit-scared about the impending reports. Even the vision of Om did not give me any respite. Everyone around me was trying to keep me in good spirits by evading the topic. Again I was tossing and turning whole night. Sleep had become an enemy from the day I realised about these hormonal issues. I woke up again around sunrise (let me also share that I had read that cancer patients should have vitamin D, so I was selfishly paying my respects to the sun god although I was always in the habit of waking up after 7 a.m.) and went to the balcony to look at the morning sun. The OM symbol was clearly embedded in between my eyebrows, and I could see the Om outlined on the sun's surface with my open eyes. The feeling of despair about the impending reports seemed to dissolve momentarily in that vision.

My parents, my brother and his wife, and my sister all accompanied me to the hospital. I could sense that they were undergoing emotional turmoil. My husband was keeping track from Nagpur and telling me that all would be well. Although I was putting a brave front, I must confess that I was shaking in and out. The moment the report came, I almost snatched it from the pathology attendant. It read: 'Benign hyperprogestationalised endometrium showing extensive stromal decidualisation, consistent with iatrogenically induced endometrial changes. There is no evidence of hyperplasia, atypia, or malignancy.' These words, with all their complicated biological references, sounded like music to my ears. We were almost jumping with joy, and I could sense a feeling of relief from my near and dear ones' faces. I did not have cancer. I had endometrial hyperplasia and adenomyosis. The bad news was that these conditions are precursors to many diseases that could develop in the future. (ANX 5 shows that significant report, which actually made me decide on alternative and holistic methods.)

DEPARTMENT OF HISTOPATHOLOGY AND CYTOLOGY

HISTOPATHOLOGY NO: 10H 731

Name of Patient: Nath Shreya		
Age: 42	Sex: Female	Date of receipt : 25-03-10
UHID NO: 1000052803		Date of report : 27-03-10

Specimen type: Endometrial tissue

Gross description:
Received multiple greywhite soft fragments aggregating to 4 cm.

Microscopic description:

Benign hyperprogestationalised endometrium showing extensive stromal decidualisation, consistent with iatrogenically induced endometrial changes.

There is no evidence of hyperplasia, atypia or malignancy.

•••END OF REPORT••

ANX 5

Surgeries / procedure

Hysteroscopy and D&C done on 25-03-10

Patient taken in OT in supine position. GA given. under above anesthesia parts scrubbed painted and draped

EUA
PS   : Cx and vagina appear normal. No e/o polyps
PV   : Uterus ≈ 12 weeks size, freely mobile, fornices free

Hysteroscopy proceeded with 4 mm scope

IN–SITU FINDINGS
Endometrial hyperplasia seen – thickened endometrium with patches of hyperemia seen.
Both ostia visualized- normal.
No polyps seen.
D& C done.
Profuse amount of endometrium curetted out, sent for HPE.
Hemostasis achieved.
Patient stood the procedure well.

Patient Response
Satisfactory.

Status on Discharge
Hemodynamically stable.

ANX 6

Anyway, after collecting the report, we were advised to consult the doctor. Dr Leena could see that we (my mother, sister Neeta, and I) were grinning and happily chattering with her as if all was over, but we found out that the bulky uterus I had was twelve weeks in size (see ANX 6) and it was risky to continue with it. The conversation was as follows (reconstruction of the conversation that happened):

Me: Doctor, my D & C report says endometrial hyperplasia, but thank God no malignancy!

Doctor: Yes, but your uterus is almost ten to twelve weeks in size, and in such cases, we advise uterus removal.

Me: Is there any medicine which can bring the uterus back to its original size?

Doctor: No, you will have to go for uterus removal because an endometrium thickness of 23 millimetres is a risk. During D & C, a large amount of endometrium has been curetted out.

Me: Doctor, is there an alternative healing method by which this can be corrected?

[My mother and Neeta, my sister who was also accompanying me—both were trying to butt in between to ask about alternatives, like Ayurveda, homeopathy, mantra, tantra, etc.]

Doctor [showing discomfort]: No, in medical science, with
  a bulky uterus of this size, we suggest removal only.
  It is risky . . .

Me: Menorrhagia is a problem, but is there a risk of cancer?

Doctor: To remove discomfort and the associated effects due
  to blood loss, I suggest you get a hysterectomy done.
  We can keep the ovaries. You already have two kids,
  and you are post–family planning age, so it will be
  of no use carrying on with this. Also you will be
  back to your regular routine in a couple of days.

Me: Okay . . . so what I do next?

Doctor: We can plan for the surgery immediately. Let me
  know how long you are in Mumbai.?

Me: Doctor, is it possible that I go back to Nagpur and come
  back to Mumbai after settling things at home?

Doctor: Okay, I am writing this prescription. You will start
  with these injections—once a month for three
  months. I am also writing iron and calcium that
  you need to take. Decide on a date, and inform me.

Me: Thank you, Doctor.

She had suggested uterus removal. In some ways, she was
right as the bleeding episodes were making my immune
system weak. It sounded like a simple procedure, and it
seemed that I was unnecessarily trying to retain something

which actually is of no use (according to medical fraternity, the organ was not of any reproductive use as I was now past child-bearing age). The doctor said, 'You are already a mother of two children, and it is only giving you problems, so prepare yourself.' And I was to let her know when I would opt for surgery. She prescribed injections to be used once a month for three months.

Anyway, we thanked the doctor and proceeded home. On the way, we visited a temple at Andheri (a location in Mumbai) and offered prasad (a food item that is offered to the religious deity and then consumed after worship). I told my family members that because the diagnosis was not very negative, I would try alternative healing methods. They were affirmative and supportive although when I checked with them later, they had their own doubts also.

The next day, I was on a flight to Nagpur. I was thinking that if any organ of the body was irritated and, instead of solving the reason for irritation, we went and irritated it further, then there was a strong possibility that it could cause a major irritation. Say, a small dust particle got into your eye. Instead of just simply washing your eye and giving it some rest, you got panicky and started rubbing your eyes, put some off the shelf ointment and rubbed the eye so much that it turned out to be a medical emergency. I was wondering why the medical fraternity was not informing us about the ways to save the uterus. If diagnosis was not cancer, then one had to look at the matter from various angles. In my case, where I had no history of irregular menstrual cycle or any type of hormonal imbalance and I was in forties, then there should be a chance given to bring the uterus back to shape.

Some of them would justify that the organ had no role to play in the post-fertility period. I felt that all organs had feelings and interconnection with various parts of the body and that removing one organ was definitely going to cause withdrawal symptoms. Say if anyone had severe problems in the eyes, then doctors have evolved methods to save the eye. They wouldn't say, 'You already know how the world around you looks like, so just get it removed.' In medical science, saving the organ had been applied in most of the cases like heart, eyes, brain, etc. But when it comes to organs like uterus, kidneys, pancreas, etc., there needed to be more research and guidance to bring them back to their regular functions through alternative methods of detoxification or rejuvenation or regeneration.

Armed with this realisation, the first thing that I did after reaching Nagpur was to search out for an Ayurvedic practitioner of repute. In India, the first thing that comes to our mind is Ayurveda because our ancestors believed and practised it, although I have always been allopathic dependent for all the healthcare decisions, like in fever, chicken pox, headache, etc. Baidyanath Group is a well-known group established in 1917 and is a brand of Ayurvedic practices and medicines. It belongs to Nagpur, and the owner Mr Suresh Sharma, a family friend. So I gave a tinkle to him, and he introduced me to one of his seasoned panel doctor, Veena Deo, and his daughter-in-law Shruti, who headed the Baidyanath Life Sciences Spa and Natural Clinic.

I started with Ayurvedic medicines in April and, also along with it, went for a detoxification procedure comprising of massage, enema, *basti*, steam baths, *nasyam*, and *garbhashay basti.* This treatment is also called panchakarma, and the doctor had designed the detox for my current condition. I felt energetic and light, but I was still having my regular doses of panic attacks, night sweats, weight gain, and 'missed' periods and 'prolonged periods'. When I had no respite coming completely from Ayurvedic treatment, then again I started contemplating uterus removal. Whenever I was depressed and anxious about menorrhagia, the nagging thought was that I was taking risk. At that time, family members sometimes supported the decision of alternative healing and sometimes advised surgery.

It had been two months since I had started Ayurveda, and the next step was to be taken. The USG of 3 May 2010 showed a bulky uterus with 15-millimetre endometrium. There was some improvement in endometrium thickness only (see ANX 7).

Now homeopathy was left to be tried. I earlier had a positive experience with treatment in the Healix Centre, a homeopathy clinic of repute at Nagpur, for treatment of chronic ailments that some of the family members had suffered, like bronchitis, anxiety, etc. It was here that I learned about mineric therapy, which is an offshoot of homeopathy.

Dr Farwah Hussain, an elegant homeopathy doctor from Healix, explained to me that hormonal imbalance can cause swelling of the uterus. She assured me that I have to be ready for almost a year's treatment and if the situation does not improve, I could go ahead with the surgery. The word is *patience.* If we are in a hurry to absolve all our health issues, then we might not be able to give space to our treatment to show its effect. Diseases like diabetes, blood pressure, bulky uterus, etc. do not come into our lives suddenly, and they are also resultant of our lifestyle, food habits, attitude towards situations in day-to-day life, so I had to flow with the treatment.

Name of Patient: -Mrs.Shreya

Ref By   Self .

Date:-   3-5-10

SONOGRAPHY OF PELVIC REGION

-The urinary bladder is well distended and is normal in
 contour & capacity.
-No intraluminal mass or calculus is seen.
The uterus is mildly enlarged and bulky (110x68x53mm).
Myometrium shows coarse echogenicity showing very
small ill defined hypoechoeic areas . .
 No obvious fibroid is noted ..
 Endometrial echoes are thickened (15 mm) and regular ..
 The cervix appears normal.
-Rt. ovary measures   31x19mm..
-Lt. Ovary measures   26x20mm.
 Both the ovaries are normal in size and location .
 Parametria are clear ...
-There is no evidence of adnexal mass .
 No free fluid is noted in cul-de-sac

*Opinion: - Mildly enlarged and bulky uterus showing coarse
           myometrium…. …suggesting adenomyosis .
           Thickened endometrium .*

ANX 7

She also told me to continue with some Ayurvedic syrups that increased iron. In between, there were bleeding episodes, and those were managed by having allopathic medicines.

I started the treatment in July 2011, and it helped me to manage menorrhagia, but the bulky uterus remained. Once in a while, some spotting happened up to December 2012. Throughout this period, Doctor Farwah advised me to have positive thoughts and somehow fool the uterus in either reaching menopause or to help the body regain regular cycles.

Now when I reflect back, I feel that uterus removals are happening so much and that the time required for these methods to give results is considered a risk.

I started further googling on the parts of the uterus and functions of ovaries. In fact, all terminologies that I came across, I started reading about them. I advise you to take this path of at least becoming knowledgeable about the condition that you have in hand. The chapters in this book will reduce your search as most of it has been compiled and explained.

Along with mineric therapy, my journey on the food that affected the hormones was also taking shape. I learnt that oestrogen was dominant and progesterone was low in my body during this disease.

I also took natural progesterone supplements from the radish family, which my father had suggested when I had asked him to search for progesterone-rich foods on the Internet. It was an all-natural, non-toxic herb.

My logic was that if ovulation was disturbed and hormones were going awry, then what should I do to balance it out? If oestrogen was dominant, then at least let me starve the body of other sources of oestrogen, and that was by not eating foods rich in it. Also if progesterone was lacking, then why not add to it by eating a diet rich in it? Along with this, I started doing pranayama and Surya namaskar (explained in Chapter 5). These are not very rigorous exercises, and they help in balancing the endocrine glands.

The USG scans on 24/2 /11 showed the endometrium at 17 millimetres (ANX 8); on 25/4/11, 8 millimetres (ANX 9); on 12/10/11, 8 millimetres (ANX 10); on 6/4/12, 18.4 millimetres (ANX 11). This shook my confidence again, and I increased my meditation tenure from forty-five minutes to one hour and thirty minutes. Also, I started doing sun salutation exercises every day without fail.

The menorrhagia had been controlled, so I had some hope. But then I was not cured, so I was again contemplating reconsidering my decision. Dr Farwah asked me to just have more patience.

Name of Patient: - Mrs   Shreya

Ref By: -   Self

Date: 24-2-11-.

USG OF   PELVIS .

The urinary bladder is well distended and is normal..
 No intraluminal mass or calculus is noted.
The uterus is mildly enlarged and bulky (105x63x55mm)
Myometrium is coarse
A small hypoechoeic area involving fundus portion .(5x4.5mm)
..............? early gestational sac .
Endometrial echoes are 17 mm thick and regular .
Cervix is normal.
Rt ovary measres   27x17 mm .(normal)
Lt ovary is enlarged,showing cystic area (28x21mm)
Parametria are clear
No free fluid is noted in cul de sac ...
 Both the iliac regions are clear .

Imp : Enlarged and bulky uterus showing changes of adenomyosis with
*   thickened endometrium .*
*   A small hypoechoeic area noted in fundus portion.......*
.   *..........? Early gestational sac*
*   Adv Follow up after 15 days .*

ANX 8

Name of Patient: - Mrs Shreya

Ref By: -   Self

Date: 25-4-11

USG OF PELVIS.

The urinary bladder is well distended and is normal..
No intraluminal mass or calculus is noted.
The uterus is enlarged and bulky (114x62x54mm ,)
No evidence of focal mass or fibroid
Endometrial echoes are 8mm thick and regular
Cervix is normal.
Rt ovary is enlarged, showing a cystic area 48x38mm).
Lt ovary measures 30x 19 mm.
Lt ovary is normal in size and location.
Parametria are clear
No free fluid is noted in cul de sac ...
Both the iliac regions are clear.

Imp: Mildly enlarged and bulky uterus
Rt ovary shows a cyst (48x38 mm).

ANX 9

Name of Patient: -Mrs   Shreya

Ref By   Self .

Date:-   12--10-11

SONOGRAPHY OF PELVIC REGION

-The urinary bladder is well distended and is normal in
 contour & capacity.
-No intraluminal mass or calculus is seen.
The uterus is mildly enlarged and bulky (105x64x53mm).
Myometrium shows coarse echogenicity showing very
small ill defined hypoechoeic areas .
Endometrial echoes are 8 mm thick ,regular ....
Rt. ovary measures   28x20mm .
Lt. Ovary measures   26x19mm.
 Both the ovaries are normal in size and location . .
 Parametria are clear ...
-There is no evidence of adnexal mass .
 No free fluid is noted in cul-de-sac.

Opinion: - Mildly enlarged and bulky showing changes of
adenomyosis .

Pl correlate clinicopath

ANX 10

Name of Patient: -Mrs   Shreya

Ref By: -   Self .

Date: 6-4-12-.

USG OF   PELVIS .

The urinary bladder well distended and is normal..
 No intraluminal mass or calculus is noted.
The uterus is enlarged and bulky (105x65x55mm)
Endometrial echoes are 18.4 mm thick/regular
No focal mass or fibroid is seen . .
Cervix is normal.
Rt ovary measures- 26x20mm .
Lt ovary measures- 30x18mm .
Both the ovaries are normal in size and location .
Parametria are clear
No free fluid is noted in cul de sac ...
 Both the iliac regions are clear .

Imp : Enlarged and bulky showing thickened endometrium
   (18.4mm).

ANX 11

Name of Patient :Mrs   Shreya Nath

Reference By   Self

Dated   : 9-4-13.

SONOGRAPHY OF PELVIS .

The urinarybladder is moderately distended and normal
No intraluminal mass or calculus is seen
Uterus is normal in size ,shape and position (82x54x45mm)
N o evidence of focal mass / fibroid
Endometrium is 7.6 mm thick/regular
Cervix is normal.

Rt ovary measures 29x16mm
Lt ovary measres   25x18mm
Both the ovaries are normal in size/location

Parametria are clear.

No free-fluid seen in cul-de-sac.

Both the iliac regions are clear

OPINION: No obvious abnormality is noted in pelvis

ANX 12

This rigmarole went on and on, and much to my surprise, on 9 April 2013, the test reports unexpectedly showed normal uterus size (see ANX 12). On a positive note, I was expecting the endometrium lining to go away or for menopause to happen, and on a negative note, at the back of my mind, there was the fear of cancer, uterus removal, diseased life, death, etc. The report showed a *normal uterus size*, and it was simply unbelievable. Dr Rajeev Nagi, sonographer and the proprietor of Nagi Imaging Centre, Nagpur, also shook his head in disbelief. His profession exposed him to n number of patients and n scans, and in this journey, I had a total of nine scans done.

I would like to sum it up that all treatments helped in some way or the other and chakra meditation and divine intervention took the healing process to its completion. Believe in this magic to cure yourself holistically!

The subsequent chapters will explain the merits and demerits of each therapy and would like you to not be influenced totally by my experiences but to objectively decide what can be best for you in the prevailing circumstances. Even in my case, it was difficult to zero in on what worked and what did not, but one thing is for sure, in holistic practices, you have nothing to lose. You are strengthening the immune system of your body, and even if any latent disease is going to strike you, it will prepare your body in a better way and will strengthen the disease-fighting mechanisms.

In each chapter, I have given some extra inputs to understand the therapies because I believe that you need to have basic knowledge before you begin. I require your patience and open mind while reading, and then you can decide what works best for you. Earlier in life, in the year 2003 to 2005, I had suffered from anxiety and depression and had followed a similar process and had been cured when a spark of light in my heart chakra appeared during meditation. The touch of the hand of God can happen any time. These journeys shaped the navakarma philosophy.

May healing, balance, harmony, divinity be with you.

CHAPTER 1

Navakarma for Mental Balance— Gyan or Knowledge

Know = Be = Understand

Understanding the Functions of the Uterus and the Ovaries

The very first emotions that we undergo in any type of trauma are fear, anger, depression, or stress. All these release toxins, and if we undergo this trauma for a period, then it manifests in some ailment or toxic condition. Knowledge is the first step or action that is required towards holistic healing. As I became a seeker for the gyan or knowledge about the causes, factors, symptoms, I was able to light my path and bring more understanding to my disease or condition. By this first navakarma, we need to dispel all fears. Ignorance is not at all bliss when danger is lurking around you.

I am sharing some of the data from the Internet that I had saved for my understanding. It might sound complicated in the beginning, but let me assure you, once you start matching your medical reports with these terminologies, there are not more than twenty words that we need to actually understand.

Uterus and Ovaries

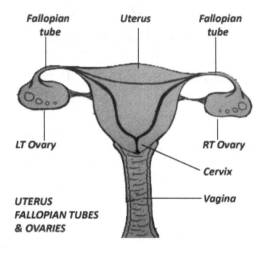

There are two ovaries, known as the right ovary and the left ovary, and they have two main reproductive functions in the body. They produce eggs for fertilisation, and they produce the reproductive hormones—oestrogen and progesterone. They undergo changes from adolescence to pregnancy to menopause and play a vital role in the fertility of every woman.

Ovaries secrete the hormones oestrogen, testosterone, and progesterone. Progesterone prepares the uterus for pregnancy and the mammary glands for lactation. Progesterone functions with oestrogen by promoting menstrual cycle.

At all stages, starting from being a girl to a woman and then old age, the oestrogen and progesterone levels keep changing. Oestrogen is primarily linked to mood swings, premenstrual syndrome, and post-partum blues. Testosterone or androgen is released in very small quantities in women.

Hormones are chemical messengers which are secreted by tissues, and they travel by way of body fluids. For the diagnosis of the level of hormones, one can get a blood/saliva test done.

We need to understand the symptoms of low and high oestrogen and progesterone because once you know that, you can plan the food philosophy that you need to follow to lower or increase a particular hormone depending on the diagnosis.

In my case, oestrogen was high, but I would like to highlight the side effects of low oestrogen so that when you know both sides, you know the level to which you need to bring the oestrogen level down and also manage food choices accordingly. My fundamental was that the body was already producing excess on its own and by the time I try finding the reasons for the same and expect my body to stabilise then why not avoid all external factors that could increase oestrogen?

Low Oestrogen

The causes for low oestrogen can be devitalised system, stress, premenopause or perimenopause, cysts, reduced functions of ovaries, etc.

Signs are sleep disturbances, fatigue, heart palpitations, depression, cold chills, etc.

Low oestrogen can be managed by:

1. nutritious diet rich in fibre and plant (*phyto-*) oestrogens—soya bean, tofu, beans, peas, fruits, vegetables
2. diet with vitamins B and C—citrus fruits, seeds, nuts
3. oestrogen-rich herbs and spices, like sesame, fennel seeds.
4. exercise for the prevention of obesity, which is important in all imbalances
5. tobacco, which can cause infertility and early menopause
6. coffee to increase oestrogen (use moderately because caffeine can have other side effects if taken in excess).

So if you have high oestrogen, then you will know from the above list of low-oestrogen foods—what has to be avoided and what has to be taken.

High Oestrogen

The causes for high oestrogen are sedentary lifestyle, stress, diabetes, genetics.

Signs are hormonal imbalance and changes in monthly cycles. During pregnancy, oestrogen level is high. Also women taking hormone-replacement therapy to control ageing also have excess oestrogen. Xenoestrogens (man-made estrogens found in plastic, cosmetics), when ingested, also increase oestrogen levels in the body. *Obesity*—especially due to consumption of processed foods, artificial colours, and preservatives—affects oestrogen levels.

High Progesterone

Progesterone also known as progestogens or progestins. It is opposite in function to oestrogen.

Causes of high progesterone are pregnancy and ovarian cysts. Pregnancy produces large amounts of natural progesterone. In a way, getting pregnant can cure adenomyosis or endometriosis but that cannot be the solution always.

Signs are irregular cycles and breast tenderness. This can be managed by increasing oestrogen so that progesterone balances itself.

Low Progesterone

Low progesterone affects your fertility the most, especially if you are in the child-bearing age. Progesterone helps the uterus or womb to thicken to receive the fertilised egg, and if it is not strong, then the baby will not be able to attach itself to the womb for the full term. Less progesterone causes maximum problems in pregnancy.

The signs are irregular or absence of monthly cycles, weight gain, depression, mood swings, thyroid dysfunction, fibroids.

Also, once you have low progesterone, there is a risk of oestrogen going high.

Oestrogen versus Progesterone

Oestrogen (the female sex hormone) dominance happens when there is too much oestrogen in the body. For most cancers, the first clinical screening involves testing of oestrogen dominance. Generally, oestrogen dominance is coupled with decrease in the hormone progesterone. Our body produces both, but because of various reasons, there is a disturbance. When we are stressed, it affects our nervous system along with our endocrine system. Our body produces both, but once there is a disturbance and if we continue taking oestrogen-rich foods, we will disrupt the endocrine system more. This can cause cancer.

Xenoestrogen and phytoestrogen are foreign oestrogen or from outside the body.

In my case, I believe excess of oestrogen could have been the cause of adenomyosis, or at least, it could have aggravated the situation. I recommend avoiding products with xenoestrogen and including diets rich in natural progesterone. This can cure conditions like bulky uterus, cysts, fibroids.

Oestrogen dominance can cause premature greying, miscarriage, breast tenderness, cold hands and feet, low libido, depression with anxiety or anger, dry eyes, early onset of menstruation, weight gain, fatigue, foggy thinking, hair loss, headaches, insomnia, magnesium deficiency, water retention/bloating, increased blood clotting, infertility, irregular menstrual cycle, irritability, premature menopause, bone loss, sluggish metabolism.

You can get a hormone saliva test to check if you are oestrogen dominant.

What Is Adenomyosis or Endometriosis?

Adenomyosis or bulky uterus or endometriosis or uterine endometriosis are synonymous to one another.

Adenomyosis is endometrium trapped within the uterine muscular wall. This causes severe pain, prolonged or excessive menstrual periods, and an enlarged uterus.

This disease was virtually unknown 150 years ago, and now it has become a mass syndrome. It is most frequently seen in women in their early or mid forties. It is due to hormonal imbalance. The uterus becomes hard and enlarged. It is generally associated with an excessive oestrogen supply. Various published studies have shown that 12 per cent of patients with adenomyosis also have been diagnosed with endometriosis in other sites outside the uterus, within the pelvis. As high as 62 per cent of women who had hysterectomy were found to have this disease on pathology reports.

What Causes Adenomyosis?

At this point in research studies, the aetiology or cause of adenomyosis is unknown.

We do know that women diagnosed with adenomyosis commonly have excess levels of the hormone oestrogen, which encourages the disease to spread monthly. A known genetic link is also present, as with endometriosis, and it does tend to run in the family.

Adenomyosis Signs and Symptoms

Bulky uterus in the ultrasonography is the first symptom. The other signs are heavy periods, painful periods, large clots, bloated feeling, backaches, abdominal pain, cramps, irregular cycles, prolonged cycles, feverish feeling, nausea, and vomiting. During the entire period, I experienced one or multiple of these symptoms.

Endometrial Hyperplasia

My histopathology report showed endometrial hyperplasia, so some description is being given so that we understand its cause.

It is a condition in which the lining of the uterus becomes so thick that it causes abnormal bleeding. It is because of too much oestrogen, and as excessive oestrogen is linked to cancer, biopsy and D & C processes are suggested to rule out the risk.

It needs medical attention. In my case, it was cured due to natural healing methods along with therapies, but in holistic cure, the individual's willpower and other preconditioning have to be taken into account.

Menopause (Cessation of Menses)

Men ('month') + *pause* ('to stop') = stopping of monthly cycles.

It is a normal event which occurs in the mid or late forties. It is a phase of life in which your reproductive cycle is over. You remain the same person as you were from your childhood to adolescence to womanhood to now, but the hype of ageing built around it is man-made.

The changes are there, but they happen over a period of time, not overnight. The entire system of endocrine glands, ovaries, thyroid, and pituitary glands undergo a change. Some unpleasant symptoms do occur to some women, such as night sweats, hot flushes, mood swings, insomnia, depression, fatigue, numbness, listlessness, headaches, backaches, and these are all due to changes in oestrogen and progesterone.

There is a risk of osteoporosis in menopause, so keeping yourself nourished is important. I followed the below diet to keep myself healthy.

- vitamin D (tablets and sunlight before 10 a.m.)
- oestrogen-rich foods, like beet juices, dark chocolate, etc. (check the list in the chapter on food philosophy)

- vitamin E
- calcium
- sprouts
- green leafy vegetables
- doing away with processed, denatured, refined foods
- increase in outdoor exercises, sleep, and engagement in work
- considering this phase as a natural phenomenon (if you are vitalised, then you will sail through this phase).

In natural menopause, the ovarian function declines gradually. In uterus/ovaries removal, the menopause is instant.

Polycystic Ovarian Syndrome (PCOS)

This syndrome is the result of faulty lifestyle, eating habits, modern-time stress, pollution, and chemicals. This syndrome has taken the form of an epidemic amongst teenagers and young women in their early twenties. It is a serious condition because it affects fertility at a young age, which can result in low self-esteem and other disorders that can affect you for a lifetime.

It is caused when oestrogen and progesterone have gone out of balance and the male hormone androgen (which is actually present in very little quantity in healthy females) increases, thus preventing ovulation, which results in multiple ovarian cysts.

If not treated on time, it can cause infertility, diabetes, heart problems, uterine cancer. Symptoms are irregular menstrual cycle, facial hair, baldness or thinning of hair on the scalp, weight gain around the waist, skin pigmentation, acne, sleep disturbances, etc.

In this condition, natural treatments of navakarma will help in removing the toxic condition, thus helping the healing process.

Disclaimer: Please note these articles have been compiled from the Net. The author has put her understanding and reproduced it in this chapter for understanding purposes.

CHAPTER 2

Navakarma for Nutritional Balance— Khaan or Food Philosophy

Detoxification = Nourish = Energy

NOURISHMENT BALANCE

This philosophy finds its roots in the statement made in the Puranas (Hindu religious texts): 'Jaisa ann waisa mann.' It literally means 'What you eat so you become in your nature.' Your body and soul will take on the type of food and water you take in. Even the type of water you drink influences your voice and general well-being. Life energy is derived from food.

Hippocrates, the father of medicine, said, 'Nature cures, not the physician.' He was a great believer of dietary measures and prescribed light diet during acute illness and liquid diet for fevers and wounds.

Also all of us have seven bodies, and the physical body and the mind are greatly influenced by the food that we eat. Besides hydrogen, carbon, oxygen, nitrogen, our body has calcium, phosphorous, potassium, sulphur, sodium, magnesium, and chlorine. There are other trace elements, like copper, selenium, iodine, etc. which are less than 1 per cent. Imbalance occurs due to excess or deficiency of any of these in our body. Healthy diet has to have variety of foods from our natural environment.

In the case of enlarged uterus, food detoxification is a key influencer because excess oestrogen and low progesterone are already playing havoc inside the body, and to counteract it, we need to totally change the food intake in such a manner that the food is rich in progesterone and deficient in oestrogen. In the list given below, I am sharing the food regime that I follow from time to time. Also, please note that you can alter it with natural foods available in your country. I am a vegetarian, so my food choices were in the vegan domain. In case of non-vegetarians, they can supplement it with the foods which have similar elements and properties.

Also note that some of the foods to be avoided may be very healthy foods otherwise, but because they are rich in oestrogen or are blood thinners, they have to be avoided till you become normal and your symptoms are under control.

Foods that cause oestrogen dominance are listed below. They should be avoided during oestrogen dominance because you would already have enough.

1. Completely avoid refined flour (*maida*).
2. Plastic wraps used in food packaging are a major source of xenoestrogen. Avoid drinking water/ liquids in plastic bottles. Switch over to glass/steel bottles.
3. Avoid white rice.
4. Avoid sugar.
5. Avoid hydrogenated oils.
6. Avoid soya products. Many patients start with soya bean milk, flour, tofu, tempeh, etc. in their food to improve weakness level, but it causes more harm.
7. Avoid aniseed (saunf).
8. sesame seed (til).
9. Avoid red meat.
10. Avoid packaged milk, dairy products. We all know that the milch animals are injected with hormones.
11. Avoid bran cereals.
12. Avoid dried fruits, like apricots, dates, prunes.
13. Avoid coffee.
14. Avoid black and green tea, which contain phytoestrogens.
15. Avoid these herbs: oregano, black cohosh, sage, licorice.
16. Avoid chasteberry.
17. Avoid chocolates.

18. Processed foods and fast foods should be totally banned during this healing process.

19. Avoid celery, parsley, beets, apples, broccoli, cauliflower, cucumbers, mushrooms, Brussels sprouts, seaweeds, squash, cherries, sunflower seeds, olives, pears, plums, tomatoes, seaweeds, prunes, barley, wheatgerm, black eye peas, lentils, chickpeas, beans, alfalfa, peas, peppers, etc.

20. You can also put the food type in Google and check the constituents for oestrogen.

Once you have regained your health, then you can indulge in a few delights once in a while.

Foods that reduce oestrogen dominance should be consumed freely when you are hungry.

1. Consume fibrous diet in the form of fruits, vegetables, beans, legumes (dals), whole grains (wheat, ragi, bajra, oats).

2. Drink plenty of water. Try to include four to six glasses of warm water throughout the day.

3. Use Ayurvedic cosmetics of reliable brands. Most of the cosmetics have xenoestrogens.

4. Walking reduces oestrogen.

5. Cruciferous vegetables broccoli, kale, Brussels sprouts, artichokes, cauliflower, cabbage, pak choi, turnip, radish, watercress, and many more.

6. Consume pomegranates.

7. Consume raw nuts, like walnuts, almond (rich in copper, iron, phosphorous, and vitamin B_1).

8. Consume onions, garlic, chives, carrots.
9. Consume turmeric.
10. Consume yogurt and fermented foods.
11. Consume macca root.
12. Consume olive oil.
13. Consume red wine, grapes, and dark berries.
14. Consume citrus fruits.
15. Consume Indian spikenard or *jatamansi*.

Foods that increase progesterone:

1. walnuts.
2. yam.
3. wild yam found in South America/Mexico (I had MacaActive Supplements)
4. colostrum/first milk of the cow (rich in progesterone and has antibodies against various diseases)
5. banana flower
6. snake gourd or *chichinda* (rich in phosphorous, magnesium, calcium, and dietary fibre).

Avoid stress because that reduces progesterone. Avoid foods that increase oestrogen levels.

Also consume food rich in nutrients like iron, vitamin C, vitamin K.

Iron is the best nutrient for your body. Most of the diseases can be averted if you have a strong immune system, and iron ranks top on the list of nutrients that strengthens the immune system.

Fill your hunger with the iron-rich foods listed below:

1. ragi or finger millet (It is nutritive and therapeutic. It is rich in phosphorus, calcium, iron, potassium, protein, antioxidants. It is a super cereal. I took the ragi flour, roasted it, mixed it with milk, and then boiled it. After that, I added sugar candy or honey. I also added walnuts and had it twice a day during menorrhagia. Till today, I have it, but now once a week. I also make ragi laddus. It is an Indian sweet where the flour is roasted and powdered sugar is added to it with dry fruits and ghee or butter. It is made into a ball, and it has a shelf life of almost a month. For ragi pancakes, prepare the batter with ragi powder, oats, wheat flour. It can also be made both sweet (with jaggery or sugar) and salty (put some green coriander, chilli, cumin seed powder). It is a flour so you can create your own recipes and make it a healthy part of your diet.)

2. spinach

3. jaggery (in small quantities as it is heaty)

4. iron supplements.

5. milk, yogurt, and dairy products (fresh only, not packaged).

6. lime

7. cherries

8. *amla* or gooseberry juice (One berry is enough to make a cup of juice. Just remove the seed, take the pulp, grind it with water in the mixer, and drink it.)

9. aloe vera juice

10. wheat grass juice

11. pineapple juice
12. pomegranate or *anaar* juice.

Sources of essential nutrients in the vegetable kingdom include parsley, coriander (*dhania*), kale, cabbage, spinach, collard greens, asparagus, cauliflower, celery, leeks, mustard leaves (*sarson*), broccoli, lady finger, cucumber, carrots, olive oil, green chillies or paprika, cloves, lettuce, etc. But some of them like cucumbers are rich in oestrogen, so stick to the ones which do not have oestrogen.

- Dried-fruits sources are prunes, blueberries, peaches, figs, currants.
- Vitamin B_6 can be found in walnuts, whole grains, lean red meat, poultry, seafood, beans, potatoes, and fortified cereals.
- Zinc is found in pumpkin and watermelon seeds.
- Magnesium-rich foods are spinach, black beans, raw plantain, lady finger, nuts.
- Snake gourd (chichinda). This is rich in phosphorous, magnesium, calcium, and dietary fibre.

You need to know this also: increase oxygen level by doing yogic exercises, like pranayama. Liver metabolises oestrogen level, so liver detoxification is important. Increase vitamin E intake. Consume inflammation reducing foods. As I had an inflammation or swelling of the uterus, my focus was to reduce the inflammation.

Log on to www.soulspacetech.com/navakarma. Sharing some of the decoctions and home remedies that I consumed. All need not be consumed together. You can have one for two weeks and the other for next two weeks. These decoctions are a part of home remedies practised in India and are handed down by our grandmothers or ancestors and have been ignored or forgotten. Also, if consumed in moderation, these herbs and spices are harmless.

CHAPTER 3

Navakarma for Water Balance— Pan or Beverages

Quality of H_2O = Quantity of Life

Our body has 65–75 per cent water, and our brain has 85 per cent of it. We cannot survive without water. We use and lose water every day. Correct water balance creates good health. We lose water from respiration (breathing), elimination (faeces), perspiration (skin), urination (kidneys). An average adult loses 2.6 litres per day. The purity of water intake decides our health.

Aerated drinks, tea, coffee, and alcohol consume water from our body. Water is essential for metabolism, removal of toxins, digestion, and regulation of body temperature. It is indeed the elixir of life.

During my healing journey, I consumed plenty of water.

1. Drink six glasses of warm water throughout the day. Start with two glasses in the morning hours. For the

rest of the day, you can drink plain water. This is the best detoxification.

2. Warm water baths are preferable, especially warm water on the uterus area.

3. Some natural therapies recommend fasting using water and fresh juices of fruits and vegetables for a few days for symptoms that are due to debility, toxins, sedentary lifestyle, etc. Intake of nutrients in juice form gives more power to the body as all vital ingredients arc assimilated faster. Beverages should be freshly prepared.

4. Consume fresh water, which has a high level of DO (dissolved oxygen). Some river waters have high oxygen levels and medicinal properties that they accrue as they pass through herb-laden mountains and forests. The Ganges river in India passes through the densest planes and possesses antibacterial properties. Still, if sewage, pollutants, industrial effluent contaminate our waterways, then such waters will also become harmful for human consumption.

If 2–3 litres are added to our water diet, then we have to ensure pure, oxygenated intake only.

CHAPTER 4

Navakarma for Health Balance: How Allopathy Helped, Ayurveda Cleansed, Minerics Therapy Worked

Prevention = Cure

How Allopathy Helped

Modern Medicine or Allopathy is a medical practice that uses biomedicine or western medicine or mainstream medicine. The basis of this treatment is that it uses agents that produce effects different from the disease treated. The symptoms in this case are different from the symptom produced by the disease. The biggest advantage is quickness of treatment. So much research has gone into this practice that it saves life more efficiently than any other form of therapy. Along with highly scientific diagnostic tools like x-ray, scanners, devices etc it controls symptoms and alleviates discomforts.

It is based on four humour theory – Blood, Phlegm, Black and Yellow Bile and four bodily conditions hot, cold, wet and dry synonymous with earth, air, water and fire. The aim is to balance the humours by treating it with opposites.

The modern medicine was helpful in controlling bleeding and also in the diagnosis part. The D & C and ultrasound were helpful in knowing the stages of my condition during the whole process. The side effects of these diagnoses are negligible compared to the benefits.

D & C (dilation and curettage) is an important diagnosis, and this is performed under general anaesthesia. It's a *minor surgery*. D & C is a brief surgical procedure in which the cervix is dilated and a special instrument is used to scrape the uterine lining. A D & C may help diagnose or treat growths such as fibroids, polyps, endometriosis, hormonal imbalances, or uterine cancer. A sample of uterine tissue is viewed under a microscope to check for abnormal cells. It helps to diagnose or treat *abnormal uterine bleeding*. D & C report can be seen in the annexure 5 and 6

Ultrasound/ultrasonography is a safe diagnostic procedure which is helpful in seeing the changes in ovaries, cervix, uterine walls. It is safe and used for pregnant women quite often as it does not use iodising radiation, like an X-ray and CT scan do. How much is too much and side effects associated with it are not known, but still one can keep a space of two to three months between each scan.

I had a total of *nine scans* done, and all of them can be seen in the annexure 1,3,4,7,8,9,10,11,12.

I also took prescription drugs from the doctors to control the bleeding episodes. I also kept them informed and never did self-medication. The additional allopathic prescriptions can be viewed at www.soulspacetech.com (navakarma section).

Allopathy has proven effective in caesarean, laser eye surgery, heart transplants, orthopaedic surgery, etc. in a major way. As more and more patients are patronising it, this branch is flushed with money for extensive research. Also, better brains are opting for modern-medicine studies as these offer high-paying jobs, so this branch is superior in knowledge.

Allopathy has quick-recovery and life-saving treatments, but its biggest drawbacks are the side effects. You should know the extent to which you need to pop the pills.

There is a tongue-in-cheek quote which I am stating below.

> He said that the aim of *allopathy* was to poison him; of hydropathy to drown him; and of homeopathy to let him die unaided.
> (L. P. Meredith, *Every-Day Errors of Speech*)

In my case, I would say allopathy or modern medicine helped me in the diagnosis and emergency bleeding episodes, Ayurveda cleansed me, mineric therapy energised me, food mindfulness nourished me, and meditation gave me the awareness to use all these therapies in the best possible manner.

How Ayurveda Cleansed Me

Ayurveda, which literally means the 'science of life' (*ayur* is 'life', *veda* is 'science'), is an ancient medical science which was developed in India thousands of years ago.

Each of us is born with a determined constitution called prakriti or doshas or bioforces. The three constitution of prakritis are vata, pitta, kapha. All three are present in every individual. The balance of the three results in good health.

Two conditions influence their development:

a. the balance of vata, pitta, and kapha energies
b. the prenatal condition in the womb.

Once established at birth, our body type does not change!

The practitioner first checked my *naadi* (pulse). It is a kind of pulse investigation which tells you about the three doshas.

Vata. This constitutes air and ether elements. The vata controls the movement of fluids and cells through the body and controls functions of the organs, muscles, nerves, and thoughts.

Pitta. This constitutes elements of fire and water. The pitta controls the digestive, metabolic activities and temperature of the body. Pitta is higher in cancer patients.

Kapha. This constitutes the elements of water and earth. The kapha controls the organic tissues, fluids, and strength parts of the body.

In my case, pitta was slightly high. I had Ayurvedic medicines for around three months. The Ayurvedic medicines and panchakarma treatment (Baidyanth brand) prescribed to me can be obtained from www.soulspacetech.com (navakarma section).

Please do not go for self-medication as doctors have the expertise to judge your body type and symptoms and their advice is important to get real benefits.

The panchakarma treatment (*pancha* means 'five' and karma in this context is 'therapies or procedures') is Ayurveda's detoxification or purification process.

The panchakarma treatment for ten days prescribed to me is briefly explained below. It was to detoxify and rejuvenate bodily tissues and functions. In our day-to-day lives, our body and mind accumulate toxins, which cause deterioration, weakening our systems and opening the door for diseases to develop.

The Ayurvedic treatment is effective only if you follow a detoxification diet along with the treatment for the particular ailment.

1. Ayurvedic massage (circulation) was done for all ten days.
2. Enema (basti) removes putrid matter and cleanses the internals.
3. Steam baths with herbs (perspiration also helps in detox) was done for all ten days.
4. *Virechana* (purgation) removes the pitta toxins which accumulate in the liver and gall bladder with medication. It cleans the gastrointestinal tract. This I did once.

The concept of balance is the root of Ayurvedic treatment.

How Mineric/Biochemic Therapy Worked

It is a type of natural therapy.

Minerics/biochemical/tissue salt therapy

A healthy life is achieved when all cells are working properly and doing self-healing. Minerals are essential building blocks of the body.

Dr Wilhelm Heinrich Schuessler, a noted German biochemist and homeopath, gave this minerics or biochemic system to mankind, in which he showcased twelve biochemic minerals present in the cells of the human body and highlighted the fact of maintaining their balance to avoid diseases. If any of these salts were deficient in the body, then health problems were manifested. These biochemic salts are also known as tissue or cell or earth salts. Their aim is to supply the missing or deficient minerals.

In this mineric therapy, you are administering salts and minerals in order to allow optimum assimilation and utilisation of nutrients consumed in the daily diet. The aim is to correct disordered cell metabolism and protein synthesis, which is the root cause of any disease. In this therapy, highly purified and diluted biochemic salts of sodium, potassium, magnesium, and calcium are given. We consume them in our daily diet, but they are in a crude, concentrated manner, so they do not assimilate, whereas in biochemic therapy, diluted salts are given in such a manner that they penetrate the cell wall and enter the cytoplasm, where actual protein synthesis takes place. These salts correct the abnormal metabolic process that a diseased organ has at tissue level.

The treatment from mineric therapy worked for me, and I continued it for almost eighteen months till I was completely cured. I totally recommend it, and my family members and friends have also benefitted from it in cases of bronchitis, diabetes, tinnitus, anxiety, etc.

Can mineric therapy be toxic?

Since it involves natural salts, which we normally eat in our food, there is no question of toxicity. They have been found to be safe and non-hazardous.

What if more salts are being absorbed?

The body will absorb only how much is required and reject the rest. If there is deficiency, it will absorb more (or you can say *replace*), and the excess is expelled. So there is no question of overdose.

You can read more about the diseases that can result due to deficiency of the twelve salts, and you can design your healthy diet accordingly.

Benefits of biochemic therapy

1. It normalises cell health.
2. It's beneficial in assimilation of vitamins as minerals are needed for proper assimilation or absorption.
3. Treatment is in harmony with the human body as tissue salts are homogenous to the cell minerals both physiologically and chemically.
4. Therapy helps in the overall well-being by also fighting with any other latent deficiencies that have not manifested in disease form.
5. It is preventive, complementary therapy excellent for all stages and ages of human life. It can be safely prescribed during pregnancy also.
6. It also relieves from stress, irritability, depression, weakness.

These medicines are prepared in capsules and sachets and are available with the biochemic salt therapy practitioner. It is an offshoot of homeopathy, so you can check if the homeopath is practising this branch. You can also email healixmedical@gmail.com. This is the clinic which I have been referred to, and they send medicines all over India and other international locations.

CHAPTER 5

Navakarma for Body Balance— Yoga/Exercises

Union = Harmony

This chapter for me is the closest to my heart in terms of sharing my holistic-healing journey because all the clarity of standing up against the disease came as I was a regular practitioner of yoga, chakra meditation, and belief systems.

When you are ill, you are slowed down and are unable to focus on anything new to do, but let me tell you, these practices are not at all vigorous and can be done without making too many changes in your surroundings and also involve no cost. So you just need to do them to get the benefits.

The basic point to keep in your mind are to create harmony amongst your mind, body, and environment around you.

Yoga Means to 'Join' or 'Unite'

Yoga improves circulation and physical-body flexibility. I would suggest that if you have been practising any other exercises, then do them moderately. You can download and learn yoga from various websites. In India, yoga is taught freely in all temples in every residential area. Pick up three to four postures and practise them. I opted for pranayama and Surya namaskar. If there is pain in any part of your body, then use help from trained yoga experts and also inform your physician. Yoga stretches are very gentle, so you can be assured of this therapy. Two yogic practices I undertook regularly were pranayama and Surya namaskar.

A. Pranayama (yogic breathing)

This is a technique to control the breathing or life force in certain steps, which then helps an individual to control the breathing pattern. Regular practice promises longevity. It increases oxygen level in the body, which in turn removes toxins. Pranayama has its origins from deep meditation, where the body starts doing this yoga on its own, and this is my personal experience. This is a type of breathing technique that actually replicates what you actually experience when you get into very deep meditation.

I have experienced that at a certain level of dhyana, a point comes when your consciousness about breathing stops. It feels that you don't require to breathe through nostrils, and there is a natural breathing happening from somewhere. After some time, one experiences complete cessation of breathing, and then the air from your body starts coming out by reverse breathing. This same process has been replicated in pranayama. The only difference is that we are doing this in a conscious state and trying to take the benefits from displacing old air in the body because once we take fresh breaths inwards, we will be filled with renewed oxygen.

The first test for a healthy body is the ability to take deep breaths. A sick person has shallow breaths. So observe your breathing, and stay healthy.

B. Surya namaskar (sun salutation)

Surya means 'the sun god', and *namaskar* means 'to bow down or salute'. The sun is the only source of energy that controls the earth and moon. It gives life energy to our bodies, and our existence without the sun is not possible. The steps are shown in the exact sequence. You need to do all steps one by one, and that makes one Surya namaskar. Like this, you can start with three Surya namaskars and then do at least eleven per day. This is the best yogic exercise to balance the endocrine glands (adrenal, hypothalamus, ovaries, parathyroid, pineal, pituitary, testes, thymus, thyroid). All seven bodies and chakras house these glands. Most of our diseases have their origin in the malfunction of these glands. Once you learn about them, you will be able to manage your current diseases and avert future diseases. Surya Namaskar is the only exercise I felt I could do during menorrhagia, and it is not exerting at all; in fact, it is more of stretching.

C. Mudras (Sanskrit word meaning 'gestures made with hands or fingers')

It is a developed form of yogic posture in which senses are primary and prana, or life force, is secondary. Hand mudras regulate the five elements in the following manner:

- thumb for fire
- index finger for air

- middle finger for space
- ring finger for earth
- little finger for water.

Maintaining balance of the five elements is important, and if there is a disturbance, we become unhealthy. When internal glands and organs become irregular or dormant, then mudras awaken them. You can practise them for ten to fifteen minutes any time anywhere.

Annexure Hand Mudras

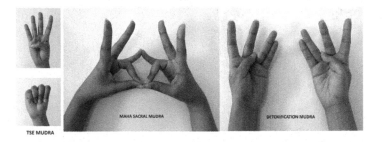

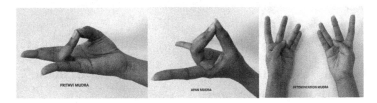

CHAPTER 6

Navakarma for Spiritual Balance—Dhyana or Meditation: Self-Healing through Chakra Meditation, Belief Systems

Silence = Strength

Chakra Meditation or Chakra Dhyana

Chakra dhyana is a very ancient meditation technique which took birth in India and later on spread in the entire world. Mankind has been searching for peace. The opposite of peace is stress, sorrow, suicidal tendencies. Just like a doctor gives the medicine to remove sickness, similarly if you find the root cause of your suffering, then you can achieve solutions. But how do we find the root cause when we are used to external help? You can be your own healer through meditation.

The basic question everybody asks me is how to meditate. The real problem is not how to meditate but the intention.

This curious tribe has the problem of sitting or lying down even for ten minutes for meditating, but if they are put in front of a TV program that's not to their liking, they will watch it for some time or even spend hours watching meaningless breaking news and episodes. It's a question of willpower and interest.

Meditation is not any specific process. It is just being yourself with yourself, watching yourself, uniting with yourself.

It is a self-realisation which opens extraordinary dimensions about human awareness. The mind thinks a lot. It knows a lot. It can create even artificial intelligence, but if you need to know beyond this mind, then meditation (specifically chakra meditation) is a fantastic tool. As we spiritually ascend, a transformation takes place within (outside in), and you develop optimum energy, equanimity, balance, discipline, and integrity.

Before we start meditating, we need to understand two things.

1. *Beej or seed mantra* is a sound vibration with mystic properties. This seed mantra, when repeatedly chanted, grows into a protective tree around you called meditation from which you can draw energy to heal.

2. *Chakras or wheels or disks or spirals* are energy nodes or points that are rotating in a circular manner like wheels inside your body. There are seven major and several minor wheels which are rotating with a certain frequency. They do not have any physical

existence (i.e. if the body is cut open, you cannot see them). These seven energy centres are where our massive nerves and organs are located.

When you speak the beej mantra, you resonate with the energy of the corresponding chakra, which will, after regular practice, start rotating in the desired manner. If chakras are blocked, disease manifests. So if you practise regular meditation, you can release those negativities that are coming your way in your daily life and let the chakras balance.

It needs regular practice, and the whole benefit is only seen when you are regularly practising it. It's like building on your energies on a daily basis. It is like any other type of study. If you are a first-time author and you write a good piece, once you taste the nectar of words, then you can write several masterpieces. So as in every study, you need to practise daily and forever.

Just begin from where you are right now. You can pick up a favourite devotional song, any chant that you like, or you can also start with the healing imbalance CD (guided meditation programme) explained in subsequent chapters.

A point will come when you are not the body, mind, ego, beliefs, bundle of emotions, intelligence but an aware soul full of truth, purity, peace, joy and connected to the highest possible source where you know not criticism, judgement, anger, hostility, needs, wants, depression, weakness, stress, or any other malady.

You are just a pure, vibrating energy particle throbbing with joy and full of light!

This energy can be felt in your palm, fingertips, feet, crown area . . .

Why Meditation?

'Why should I meditate? Why not just go for a long walk or chill with my friends or go clubbing, dancing, chatting, etc.? That also will distract my mind and give me relief.'

Ask yourself whether the momentary distraction will permanently solve your problem. If yes, then the problem is not a *problem*.

There is a point where your human strength fails you, especially in terms of health, relationships, worldly worries, and traumatic experiences beyond your control, like terrorism, natural disasters, etc.

If our computer is getting attacked with a virus, wouldn't you go all out to save it from the crash?

We might have strength of character, healthy body, sufficient wealth, but sometimes events in your life break you. The wisdom that spirituality gives you helps in seeing your difficulties as transient. Life has dualities. We all are alternating between sorrow and happiness, gain and loss, etc., and they are cyclic. Meditation is a communion with the higher self. You give up in order to go up and then receive transformation.

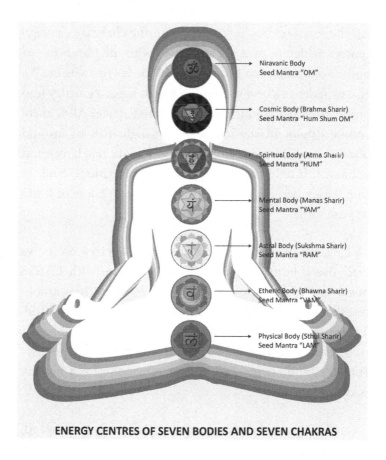

ENERGY CENTRES OF SEVEN BODIES AND SEVEN CHAKRAS

Also, it does not happen in one day. Yes, transformation can happen in less than a second, but you have to offer yourself to the source. After this, when the same things trouble you, it won't matter because your reaction towards them has changed.

Every religion has discovered paths to liberation. Choose yours. Also, add new dimensions from your discoveries.

All the seven bodies have a link with the chakras or energy centres, which in turn are associated with the glands in our body. Meditation is a process to feel the energy within. We also experience a new dimension which is not a journey into outer space but a journey in our inner space. Also, there comes a point in the journey when light fills us up and bodily corrections start happening. It does not happen at your will. It only happens to a regular practitioner and, in some cases, because of divine intervention. It happens faster to pure souls.

'Why activate the chakra? Can't we just carry on as we are?' Every human being is born in nature with certain positives and negatives. Every chakra has two sides to it—one that nature has bestowed and one that you have to find. The earlier you begin in this lifetime, the easier will be the transformation. Remember, chakras control all aspects of your life, and energy has to flow efficiently for a healthy body and mind.

As chakras open the energy centres, your body get cleaned, and there is a tremendous feeling of joy.

First, we need to understand chakra and our body and the placement of chakras and associated organs so that when we do meditation, we are fully involved and are witness to the happenings in a more realised manner.

We have seven bodies and seven chakras (refer to the diagram).

1. The physical body (*sthul sharir*) is the body that you see through the naked eye. The first seven years of human life are spent in nurturing the physical body. The other bodies are in seed form. The corresponding chakra is muladhara chakra, also known as root chakra, which is the starting point or the beginning of the central nervous system or spinal cord. Sex is the natural possibility, and once transformation happens, then *brahmacharya* (celibacy) is the transformation of this chakra. The beej mantra or primordial sounds mentioned in Vedic text is *lam*. The colour is red. The repetition (minimum of 108 times) on specific time in a day for a certain period of time—say, twenty-one days—will start activating this chakra. The benefits are that all suppressed feelings obstructing you will be unleashed. The ovaries, testes are the glands associated, and hormones are oestrogen, progesterone, testosterone. Animals develop only in the physical body.

2. Etheric body (*bhawna sharir*) is the body that makes you feel love, anger, hatred, passion. Humans spend seven to fourteen years in this body, where emotional, sexual growth takes place and the physical body also grows. Half of the human species is forever stuck in this. The corresponding chakra is *swadhisthana*, located a few inches above the root or muladhara chakra. The beej sound is *vam*. The

colour is orange. The natural emotions are fear, hate, anger, violence, and the transformation is love, compassion, fearlessness, friendliness. The gland is the adrenal glands, located above the kidneys. The hormones are adrenaline, cortisone, and many more.

3. Astral body (*sukshma sharir*) is the body that enables you to reason, think, and apply intelligence. Humans spend fourteen to twenty-one years in this body. Many people reach only up to this level in their lifetime. The chakra is manipura, and the natural emotions are doubt and thinking, which transform into trust and intelligence once the chakra is activated. This chakra is located just above the navel. The gland is pancreas. Pancreas release glucagon and insulin. The beej sound is *ram*. The colour is yellow. The activation of this chakra helps you to be more decisive. Decision comes from a state of clarity which is beyond thoughts.

4. Mental body (*manas sharir*) helps you to reach your highest possible goals with the talents that you have acquired. The singer will absorb more and create new music; the lawyer will bring new dimensions to his profession. Humans spend their age twenty-one onwards in this body. The *anahata*, or heart, chakra activation converts your imagination to determination and daydreaming to vision. The thymus gland is located in the anahata (or heart) chakra. It produces thymosins. The beej sound is *yam*. The colour is green. Psychic vision is developed.

5. Spiritual body (*atma sharir*) is the fifth body, which
    comes into play if your growth in life has continued
    in a proper manner. By age thirty-five onwards,
    if you start experiencing soul consciousness and
    enlightenment, then you can be an active seeker
    for enlightenment. The *vishuddhi* chakra (throat
    centre) gets activated, and you are rid of pain, hatred,
    jealousy, desires. The glands are the parathyroid
    (regulates calcium) and thyroid. The beej sound is
    hum. The colour is blue. As you are awakened, you
    can see what you have been thinking.

6. Cosmic body (*brahma sharir*)—this plane can be
    reached by the seeker once consciousness no longer
    belongs to him/her. The *agya* chakra located
    between the two eyebrows, also known as third eye,
    gets activated, and the seer rises above the body and
    self. The ideal age is forty-two to forty-nine years.
    The beej sound is Om. Also *hum*, *sum*, Om in some
    texts. The colour is indigo. The enlightenment and
    awakening have begun for the seeker.

7. Niravanic body—explaining the sixth and seventh
    body is meaningless because once god realisation
    or total liberation occurs, there are no words to
    decipher it. The chakra is *sahasrar* or crown, and
    this houses almost all the glands that are associated
    with the human body functions (pituitary, pineal,
    hypothalamus). They together produce more than
    a dozen hormones and might be more. They also
    are responsible for regulating the production of
    other hormones of other glands in the body. So
    in a way, crown chakra or sahasrar hold the key to

the endocrine glands. The beej sound is *Om*. The colour is violet and diamond white.

When you speak the beej or seed mantra, you resonate with the energy of the corresponding chakra, which after regular practice, starts rotating in the desired manner. If chakras are blocked, disease manifests. So if you practise regular meditation, you can release those negativities that are coming your way in your daily life and let the chakras balance.

A Brief Outline of Energy Flow During Meditation

Nadis pathways or channels carry the life force or prana in our body. Yoga nadis are thousands of conduits through which pranic force emits.

The Shiva samhita treatise on yoga states, for example, that out of 350,000 nadis, 14 are particularly important and amongst them, the three just mentioned are the most vital.

- *Ida* is associated with lunar energy. The word *ida* means 'comfort' in Sanskrit. Ida has a moonlike nature and feminine energy with a cooling effect. It courses from the left testicle to the left nostril.
- *Pingala* is associated with solar energy. The word *pingala* means 'tawny' in Sanskrit. Pingala has a sunlike nature and masculine energy. Its temperature is heating and courses from the right testicle to the right nostril.
- *Sushumna* connects the base or root chakra to the crown, or sahasrar, chakra. Sushumna is the hollow

passage that runs through the spinal cord. This houses all the seven chakras. The sushumna ends in the *brahmarandhra*, the tenth opening in the brain. Please note the other nine openings are the one mouth, two eyes, two nostrils, two ears, one anus, one genital. So there are nine openings for men and ten for women. A ship with holes is bound to sink. Similarly, a body (ship) with impure senses (holes) is bound to doom. How can we plug these holes? Or to put it otherwise, how can we render our senses purified and sanctified? By meditating on the divine.

Once your kundalini arises, it pierces through all the chakras, and in this process, considerable amount of sexual energy gets transformed into spiritual energy, which gets stored in the brain and in turn strengthens psychic powers and vision. As it rises, the seeker attains infinite bliss.

The ida and pingala nadis are often seen as referring to the two hemispheres of the brain.

The rise of the kundalini shakti or energy gives us wisdom, self-realisation, and subconscious perceptions.

In European ancient texts, there is a similarity drawn with the three main nadis (ida, pingala, and sushumna) being related to the caduceus of Hermes: 'The two snakes of which symbolise the kundalini or serpent-fire which is presently to be set in motion along those channels, while the wings typify the power of conscious flight through higher planes which the development of that fire confers.'

How Long Does One Need to Practise?

In the initial stages, you need to practise for one hour a day and for almost a month without break. Even if you do it for ten days at a stretch, you will be able to break the resistance. Also, once you get focussed, you will undergo all varieties of emotions, like feeling delightful and then feeling sorrow. You have to let it happen. This is a part of the mind purification process.

Like any other exercise, sports, dance, or even office regime, this practice has to have a timetable in the initial stages. Once you know how to channel your energy centres, then even ten to fifteen minutes of quiet time can rejuvenate you. Also, if you are awakened, then you will be forever in meditation.

Chakra Meditation

The *Santulan* healing mantra CD/DVD has been created using ancient texts and scriptures. You can order a CD or DVD.

Santulan (Hindi word for 'balance') is a guided meditation CD/DVD for chakra balancing. It comprises of healing mantras for our well-being.

The first manifestation of the infinite spirit is through cosmic sound. *Aum* (Om) is a self-created sound of the universe. The seed/beej mantras, along with aum, creates rhythm that causes energetic vibrations which result in unity and harmony.

This CD/DVD has divine sounds of *ekakshri* (single-letter) seed mantras which correspond to the seven chakras in the body. The sound level of each word (*lam*, *vam*, *ram*, *yam*, *ham*, and *Om*) is repeated in a cycle of 108 times in a specific manner, and if it is accompanied with the colours or light associated with the respective chakra, the overall journey of moving inwards is maximised. Light and sound, which are integral parts of our being, have great connections to self-realisation. The DVD explains visually about the meditation.

This *Santulan* meditation has been conceptualised by Kamal Narayan Seetha, who has almost two decades of experience in chakra-balancing sessions.

Listening to this CD/DVD regularly helps in removing anxiety, insomnia, depression, mood swings, and stress, and it releases positive hormones, which induce general well-being.

For ordering this healing mantra CD/DVD, you can email shreya@soulspacetech.com.

Chakra Meditation for Cleansing and Strengthening Your Aura for Good Health, Happiness, and Creativity

Aura or *tejas* (in Sanskrit) or *aabha* or *prabhamandal* (in Hindi) is the halo around you, and it is a reflection of your true self. We are all a manifestation of energy. From the breaths we take to the biochemical reactions in our bodies, to the stages in all our ages, we all follow a scientific process. The imperfections in our lives distort the ideal human life span (100 years or more) at the physical, mental, and spiritual levels. The mental thoughts are soundless vibrations.

Kirlian photography detects energies emitted from human body. These energies form patterns. Studies over a period of time have made some differentiating factors that can tell us about a positive or accentuated aura and negative or depleted aura.

The following procedures help in strengthening and purifying the aura, and it has to be practised daily to experience the benefits. If you want change, then don't let complacency overpower you.

- yoga
- meditation
- prayers
- forgiveness
- having less expectations
- being less judgemental
- respect for self
- service.

Even if you are spiritually healthy but is still surrounded by negativity, you need to keep your smile so that the negative does not overpower you. In fact, I would suggest doing positive actions or karma more so that when negativity tries to overpower you, the good actions are able to combat it.

Aura can be read through specific instruments. The colour of the aura signifies the health and emotion of that specific location. Red aura is related to the physical body and benchmarks your ego status. The positive side of being red is good circulation, and the negative side is anger and an anxious temperament. Orange aura is related to etheric level and signifies energy and vitality. These colours are in line with colours shown in the diagram of energy centres of the seven bodies and seven chakras.

If creating life has a process (like the nine months of gestation, stages of development, procedure of birth followed by development from child to adult to old age), then exiting life also follows a process of shutting down of various body mechanisms, preparing for an upward movement of energy centres, slowing down of mental faculties, etc. In Hinduism, there is a strong belief of rebirth, and devout Hindus live their present lives absolving past and present karmas to be able to secure a better rebirth. The aura changes depending on life's trials and tribulations. The aura depicts the essence of the life you are currently living.

Belief Systems

We should understand that most of our suffering finds way into our mind because of certain belief systems that we have been ingrained with. The neighbour has a Mercedes, and you feel inadequate with your sedan with an inferior brand. This thought causes a slow poison or pollutant that is not tangible like a snake or mercury poisoning, which we can remove physically. Meditation or self-introspection allows us to remove these toxins mentally.

Certain norms are handed down to us from sources around us since our birth.

- parents (e.g. at dinner, they might say 'Eat as much as you can'; now even if we are not hungry, we tend eat more than required at parties because of this conditioning)
- society (e.g. women who go out to work generally tend to overlook kitchen chores and bringing up children the right way)
- religion (you must keep this fast in order to get a good husband)
- philosophy (religious philosophies on abortion, gay marriages)
- peers (once you are eighteen years of age, you cannot stay with your parents).

If you keep following your belief systems rigidly, then people around you start seeing a pattern in your behaviour.

In case of bulky uterus, my muladhara (root) and swadhisthana chakra were blocked, so I had to accept the situations and factors that were causing hostility in my body and mind and sending negative signals to these chakras. I had kept a positive acceptance statement in my purse, which I used to read on daily basis. I was sending positive energy through my mind and externally through hand to the uterus, thanking the organ for the part it had played as a womb in giving birth to two healthy and intelligent children and also for the part it will be playing in keeping my body healthy.

Say, you are having problems with your relative or office colleague, and because of that, negative hormones are being released. The belief system method helps you to accept the problematic situation and finds ways out to deal it and overcome it. Basically, you don't have to allow the emotion to take charge of you. You need to take charge of the emotion and beliefs associated with it.

Once you learn to meditate, then you are able to alter your belief systems in a better way. So we can say that to enter alternate state of mind is meditation.

While entering this alternative state, I wanted to know why I was suffering from these symptoms, and in the process of self-exploration, I came across the belief system coaching which my sister Neeta was practising.

This is what Neeta, who is a belief system expert, has to say:

Have you heard yourself saying

'How much ever I work hard I am not appreciated.'

'Life is full of struggles.'

'I have to compromise out of fear of instability.'

Did you know that these are your beliefs made during a time of stress and now these have become a pattern in your life which is repeating in an auto pilot mode? Beliefs disempower you, are the cause of lack of vision, decreased energy and engagement and ultimately this unwillingness to put in your full potential repeats the pattern.

A person is guided by his/her belief system for most part of his /her life. It is beliefs that make you think and feel the way you do and attract similar circumstances in your life. These beliefs got built into you as you absorbed them from your environment as you went through events and experiences of pleasure and pain right from the day you were born and probably even before that. Know that belief is an individual's perception that depended on how he took the event.

There is a famous Saying:

'Between stimulus and response there is a space. In that space is our power to choose our response.'

Thus we can always control our reactions to an event. But in the presence of beliefs we become powerless to our emotions and our subconscious.

Beliefs are the preset filters through which we see the world. They are like 'Internal commands' to the brain as to how to represent what is happening. They are a definition you gave to or an emotion you attached to an event or person when you evaluated it based on your reference.

If you reflect closely, you will see your belief-system at work, as reflected in your level of success, your health, wellbeing and the quality of your relationships.

There is a famous saying 'Nobody grows old. When people stop growing, they become old.' If you believe you are weak bodied, the cells of your body obey you and manifest it. If you believe you are depressed, your sense organs echo it, If you believe you are unstable, your knees go weak and If you believe no one hears you, your voice gets choked up. Thus you physically become the 'interpretation' as you internalize it.

Some examples of people's beliefs?

- If I don't eat well, I will become sick
- If I am unwell, people notice me and take care of me
- Money can't buy happiness.
- People are untrustworthy
- Getting wet in the rain causes diseases

How is my health related to my beliefs?

Research has confirmed that your beliefs about food can greatly affect how you metabolize those foods.

Some people are known to eat large portions and yet remain slim. Others barely smell the food and become overweight.

For around 30 years research has consistently shown that your beliefs are the primary determinant of health, more so than diet, exercise, genes etc.

How do I change my belief-system?

As a human being you are constantly evolving and thus your emotions, your likes, dislikes, opinions, fears etc need to be revisited. Living a life of awareness will help you watch your emotions and thoughts and catch the ones that don't apply in the moment. Meditation helps you identity your individual perceptions and release them or replace them with healthy ones. (http://www.neetasinghal com/Blog/)

For identifying your beliefs and releasing them, you may contact Neeta Singhal at neeta.singhal@rudracentre.com, and her website is www.rudraksha-ratna.com.

CHAPTER 7

Navakarma for Social Balance— Kaam or Work: Take Charge of Your Life through This Karma

Work = Transformation

Work is the best tool to recharge your mind. All great sages, men, women who have walked this earth (like Lord Buddha, Swami Vivekananda, Mahatma Gandhi, Nelson Mandela, Mother Teresa, etc.) have showed that karma yoga (the path of worship through work) is accomplished by doing, moving, walking, and playing the game of life. None of them ever rested till their last breaths.

During any of the sickness or problems, I did not stop going to my office or doing other chores until and unless it was not manageable. In my case, I have my own organisation, so I could have done work from home and managed, but being a follower of karma yoga, I was at my workplace during my anxiety, depression, and hormonal imbalance stages and kept taking the necessary rest and medications in between. Being at work distracts your mind and helps you to heal.

Also chasing targets, talking to people, creativity, etc. keep your mind positive.

Bhagavadgita (a Hindu scripture also known as Song of God) states, 'You have the right to work, but never to the fruit of work.' Keep doing things with no expectations because if expectations are not met, then you will have pain. Pain will make you unhealthy.

The late A. P. J. Abdul Kalam, president of India, was a true karma yogi, and he states, 'All Birds find shelter during a rain. But Eagle avoids rain by flying above the Clouds.'

CHAPTER 8

Navakarma for Emotional Balance—
Daan or Charity: Giving Is Living

Sharing = Grace

All problems have their origin in the cause–effect theory. Similarly, all karma or actions follow Newton's principle of action and reaction. An act of noble deed will enrich your soul in such a way that ultimate emotional balance is reached.

If the benefit is in the mind, then charity will be selfish or a business transaction. Charity can be done in various forms by giving food, clothes, medical care, knowledge, organ donation, land, cow, money, etc.

The greatest of all daan is *abhaya* daan, where you do not raise any fear in any living being, not even the slightest. *Abhaya* in Hindi means 'free from fear'. This charity emphasises on being protective of all living beings and having the ultimate compassion.

Supreme charity lifts the nature of the giver. A Hindu
proverb sums up the essence of charity.

> Living creatures get influenced through dānam,
> Enemies lose hostility through dānam,
> A stranger may become a loved one through dānam,
> Vices are killed by dānam.

CHAPTER 9

Navakarma for Holistic Balance— Saam or Advice and Assimilate

Action = Reaction = Learning

Repetitive Action = Mastery over Learning

When all eight navakarma principles are assimilated, applied, imbibed as a part of our daily routine, then you can be a master of a healthy body, mind, and spirit with fantastic energy levels, youth, and longevity.

According to the great Indian teacher, philosopher, royal advisor to the emperor Chandragupta called Chanakya (371 BC to 283 BC), there are four ways to make someone do a task.

- saam—to seek advice
- daam—to offer a price and buy
- *dand*—to punish and get it done
- *bhed*—to exploit the weakness or secrets.

A child not willing to study even after a lot of advice (saam) may be offered a toy or sweet (daam) to finish the homework, and if he still does not do it, then the parent will exercise their control by not allowing the child to watch cartoon shows for two weeks as a punishment (dand). In extreme cases, they might take away the favourite toy car and give it back only once the homework is completed (bhed).

Navakarma of mental balance (gyan) and holistic balance (saam) are already in application by you as you have already taken the first step of seeking knowledge.

Advice is available for almost all your problems, but the seeker has to be consistent in using the advice. In case of meditation to actually happen, one cannot see the real benefits if the seeker does it irregularly. An obese person will be able to see the results of the gym routine only after two to three months of regular practice. The food practice has to enter your list of items that you buy from the grocery and fruit/vegetable vendor in real.

Make a Difference to Your Body, Mind, and Soul

The body has self-healing properties; otherwise, the external wounds, fractures, headaches would not have healed at all. Surgeons will also agree that post surgery they wait for the patient to heal. From time immemorial, self-healing and even healing by others have been accepted. In modern times, although we have abundant knowledge on autosuggestion, spirituality, various healing techniques, we lack the patience and courage to lead a disciplined life.

When all body organs, blood, mind are synchronised or purified, only then can healing have a conducive environment to show its effect. Sunshine and oxygen combined with foods that convert into energy will nourish the physical body. Good thoughts will nourish the mind. Increase your willpower. The greater the will, the more the flow of life force or prana.

We might have a nose, but what instructs the nose to breathe even without our conscious or subconscious instructions? That one thing is our supreme soul.

Soulful Musings

We know that the soul is neutral, indestructible, boundless, and immortal, but what does it have to do with the karmas of the physical, etheric, astral, mental, spiritual, cosmic, nirvanic bodies?

An ordinary face can possess a beautiful soul, and an ugly soul can have a charming face. The soul has no physical appearance.

Bad and good souls are two of a kind. Sages possess a divine soul, and a tyrant possesses a depleted soul. In a pure soul, the conflicts are resolved, and in an impure one, they rule the mind and body.

One soul can make a difference to many in a positive way. Nelson Mandela and Mother Teresa made a difference to humanity; Albert Einstein and Isaac Newton to science; Jesus Christ, Gautam Buddha, and Prophet Mohammad to worship and religion; Mahatma Gandhi to a nation. Similarly, one soul can make a negative impact to many. So souls can be creators or destroyers.

The soul needs a physical body to manifest itself, and to survive, it also uses oxygen, water, food, blood, plasma, etc. The soul needs breath, light, energy.

The mind learns religious preaching. So a Hindu mind creates a Hindu person or body, but an awakened soul merges into eternity, which does not have these boundaries. The mind is Hindu, Muslim, Buddhist, or Christian.

When you speak the truth, the soul knows, and when you lie, the soul hears.

Greed, anger, jealousy, hatred make the soul restless.

Charity, happiness, love, warmth make the soul peaceful.

Whether we are asleep or awake, the soul is always active.

The soul seeks pleasure and bliss for which it uses the heart and mind.

Some memories strengthen the soul, and some dissipate it. The soul watches these memories.

Does the soul play its part or only watches the play?

The soul is energy. It is life. The soul is neutral when we are born. The mind and heart feed it with experiences of goodness and adversities. If there is a change in the heart and mind, then you can change from impurity to purity.

The soul cannot live forever inside the body. One day it has to leave. So activate and develop your soul in this life. True healing originates from a developed soul as this soul is part of God.

Navakarma is leading a soulful life with common sense.

I am sharing a poem penned down by me.

Soul Is the Reflection of God

If the mind is pure
The heart flourishes
If the heart is clean
The mind beams
The soul shines in the purity of the heart and mind
Depression, disease, and death emerge from
the impurity of the mind and heart
Develop your soul in this life, and experience true healing.

Holistic Flow Chart for Uterus Diseases/ Take Charge of Your Body/Optimise Yourself

I am including an easy flow chart for you to follow. Also, you should design your holistic-healing program according to your country, food types available, religious upbringing, and alternative therapies that have yielded results. The disorders that impact the menstrual flow are systemic in origin, and they should be handled by treating the system as a whole. First, remove toxicity, build general health, and then treat.

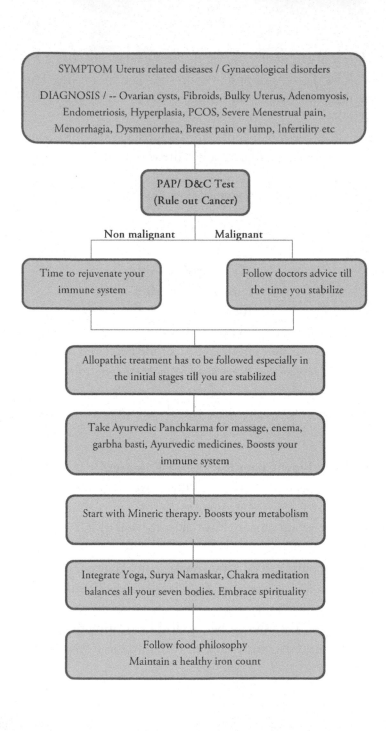

SYMPTOM Uterus related diseases / Gynaecological disorders

DIAGNOSIS / -- Ovarian cysts, Fibroids, Bulky Uterus, Adenomyosis, Endometriosis, Hyperplasia, PCOS, Severe Menestrual pain, Menorrhagia, Dysmenorrhea, Breast pain or lump, Infertility etc

PAP/ D&C Test
(Rule out Cancer)

Non malignant   Malignant

Time to rejuvenate your immune system

Follow doctors advice till the time you stabilize

Allopathic treatment has to be followed especially in the initial stages till you are stabilized

Take Ayurvedic Panchkarma for massage, enema, garbha basti, Ayurvedic medicines. Boosts your immune system

Start with Mineric therapy. Boosts your metabolism

Integrate Yoga, Surya Namaskar, Chakra meditation balances all your seven bodies. Embrace spirituality

Follow food philosophy
Maintain a healthy iron count

All the healing procedures will balance the metabolism and strengthen the body, and in no way can they cause any harmful effect. Sun, water, air are available around you. The quality of water and air you can change only to some extent, but food and dietary habits are influenced by your choices, so you need to follow the correct food plan. Remember that you yourself are putting food in your body through your own hands. So be responsible about it.

In case the report says malignancy (cancer then), still gather courage to follow the above routine along with the treatment prescribed by your medical experts. You can support your healing process by following the above. With strong tissues, body fluids, vitamins and minerals, you will rejuvenate.

Take Charge of Your Body

Your physical body is a reflection of your inner thoughts, food habits, and genes.

Sometimes even when you are following a fitness-and-food regime, some diseases can strike us. External factors, like pollution and chemicals in the food, are beyond our control.

Menopause is not a disease. It is a time of your life which needs to be understood.

Similarly, hormonal imbalance is also an outcome of stress, emotional changes, trauma, fear, etc. It happens to everybody but gains out of proportionate when we refuse to know our body. From childhood to adolescence, to marriage followed by pregnancy, then up to menopause, you need to just be aware of five important fundamentals.

1. *Detoxify*. Use the body but also clean it. Give it sunshine and food supplements that can add vigour to your system.
2. *Exercise*. Improve circulation, reduce excess weight, and increase your energy levels.
3. *Be occupied*. Keep educating yourself, working on the profession or interests that you have. Homemakers (housewives) should engage in doing some household chores themselves as it keeps them fit and also saves money. If you are self-empowered and confident, then you are an inspiration to family and friends in your society because of your positive mindset.
4. *Me Time*. Take out a minimum of half an hour and a maximum of one hour for your hobbies, interests, meditation, and self-introspection.
5. *Family*. Spend time with family. Each member has to be treated with dignity, self-respect, understanding, and love. Self-centered individuals tend to bring disharmony in family life, so avoid being one of them.

Optimise Yourself

Every body type or individual has a role to play and journey to undertake. Although we might be on different paths, we possess similar natural environment and body mechanism. If we overuse any of our organs/abilities to the point of discomfort over a prolonged period of time, then we are stretching/stressing it. If it is not repetitive, then our natural mechanisms can heal the body, but if repetition continues, then at breaking point, disease will manifest. We should optimise all our body functions with conscious efforts. While meditating, let's see our physical, emotional, and skeletal system, and try locating areas of discomfort or pain. Once we are aware, then we can plan the course of action.

I used to sit in a certain posture while working at the office where my left elbow rested on the armrest of my chair while I was always busy typing with my right hand. I only became aware of it recently when I suddenly developed a needle-like pain in my left elbow and found it very difficult to move. The doctor diagnosed it as tennis elbow. I had acquired a tennis elbow without playing tennis! The simple way to heal it was to change the posture of the last twelve years into a different alignment, massaging coconut oil or balm, giving positive healing, rubbing the part with gentle caress, and doing exercises of tennis elbow suggested by the physiotherapist. In two months' time, it was gone. No medications, no injections. Just being aware is important.

Let's go back to days where we worked hard and had time to go for picnics, outdoor activities, retreat, recreation. Now we party hard but all indoors and sometimes all alone.

Modern-day maladies, which are on rise due to overuse or overstraining, need to be tackled. They are listed below.

- hormonal disorders in males/females
- sore throat (in the name of communication, excessive talking has become equivalent to success)

- eye disorders (we have never seen so many spectacles in a classroom of a school before the year 2000 or Y2K or the twenty-first century)
- thyroid
- obesity
- excessive intake of food
- alcoholism/drugs/smoking
- anxiety/stress
- respiratory disorders
- blood pressure
- diabetes
- cancer

Relaxation Techniques/Exercises in Case You Have Not Decided to Practise Meditation/Yoga/Sun Salutation

Let's move away from meditation, and let's practise what can bring ease and relaxation. Always wear cotton and comfortable clothes, and find a comfortable position to sit on or lie down. The whole body should be in a relaxed posture. Practise the art of observing each and every body organ one by one and then feeling the blood flowing in your system, air, fluids, skin—all that which makes up your physical body. Feel each of them through your mind, and then send deeply calming energy to them. Start with your eyes then eye sockets, eyelids, eyebrows, face . . . Keep sending loving energy through your mind literally as if you were speaking to them.

Also, from your inner eye, keep observing if any part is paining or feeling uneasy. Pay attention to it. Say, if it is your throat, go back to all your activities that could have caused it. You will be able to identify it. Was it the food/drink consumed or some kind of irritant or pollution that you inhaled or emotional distress or excessive shouting?

If your earlobe is paining, then check the amount of time you spend on your mobile and which ear has been stressed out. Even patients lying down in one direction on a bed get bedsores. So your routine can reflect the cause and effect of any disease that you have recently acquired.

Once you have zeroed in on the cause, then you need to make an action plan to deal with the pain.

Also, rotating the neck and doing exercises in which all body parts are shaken (especially the blood, which has to flow to your head) should be done. Avoid strenuous exercises, and do not exert yourself. Even if you are putting on weight, I would suggest that you need to be gentle with your body. Once you heal, then you can do weight management.

How to Overcome Fear

This is a powerful energy inside us, and if not handled the right way, it can be more destructive than any physical harm.

The fear of earthquakes, terrorists in front of you, natural disasters, accidents is real, and feeling panic or anxious about them is normal. But fear of something that has not manifested in reality but has infested your mind—like a person's words or actions, thoughts of a disease that you read about, poverty, past negative experiences of yourself and others—contribute a lot to fear.

Fear is a thought that arises in our mind when we see, hear, or feel something that is perceived as a threat or danger to our lives. It is actually when we are scared of losing the power of life that we are living—say, losing a job or loved one, hunger, pain, diseases. It is the perceived loss or danger that creates fear. It is a doubtful or false feeling, but too much fear makes it look real.

As such, snakes, poisonous chemicals, terrorists, disease-causing agents exist in the environment, but fear actually does not exist. It is created by us. Chronic fear releases stress hormones, and once we are engulfed in fear, then it affects our physical, emotional, and spiritual planes.

In my case, as I was previously practising meditation for several years, even if fear attacked my physical and emotional planes, the spiritual plane helped me in thinking clearly, deciding solutions, starting fresh, being persistent, and uplifting positive searches.

Steps to Overcome Fear

Nutritional food lessens fears by releasing the happy hormones serotonin, endorphins, and dopamine. Follow a discipline like yoga, meditation, sports, or a hobby every day.

Take the time to reflect. Don't watch fear. There is a Chinese saying that there are six solutions to all your problems, so find solutions.

Keep saying, 'It is temporary. It will pass. It is just an inner condition.'

Rearrange your energy pattern by distancing yourself from all negative people, emotions, news, and images.

Remember, no one else can take charge of your fear. Take charge of it yourself.

Health Tips for Women Younger and Older Than Forty

Females experience more bodily changes than males because of many emotional and physical changes they undergo in their life's journey. These changes, if handled with awareness, will make the transition smooth. Another important aspect in menstrual symptoms is that generally women feel shy discussing openly about it and some feel guilty also because of social taboos. Also, many symptoms go untreated because excessive discharge, bleeding, missing periods, abdominal cramps, etc. are taken very lightly, and generally, many productive days and sometimes years go away while managing the after-effects of the syndrome. Everybody undergoes it, so you have to also manage it. It is in the attitude.

It is a natural process, but abnormal symptoms have to be recognised and brought under control. The first thing you must do is make a list of symptoms that affect you during your monthly cycle, and also put down your dates (instead of playing memory games) and ensure they are not changing drastically. Despite being busy as a working woman, I used to note down the happenings and the dates and google about each terminology in my medical report. It strengthened my knowledge on food constituents (so much so that when I eat mushroom, it is rich in vitamin B_2, riboflavin, and selenium comes to my mind). I practise what I am preaching in this book, and I'm looking forward to being a healthy human being. Being healthy is not about mere existence but the ability to resist disease, to be powerful in body and mind, to have a spring in your steps.

Before forty, during this period, you are laying down the foundation for your body so nutrition, physical activities, and nurturing good thoughts will go a long way to build a healthy constitution. The typical problems are missing periods, heavy bleeding, pains, cramps, headaches, giddiness, poor self-esteem, and in extreme cases, PCOS. None of these come into your life suddenly, and the first step is to take responsibility of your body. As you notice any changes, the first step is to discuss it with your mother, family, or relatives because they will have experiential advice. If the problem persists, then go for medical counselling to correct the problem. Also, follow the holistic flow chart described in chapter 8.

Give special attention to hygiene, exercises. Avoid fried, sugary, salty, white-flour, junk foods. Avoid drinking coffee and tea on a daily basis. Set small achievable career or life goals. Anxiety, depression, and fear of failure play havoc with your hormones. Wear cotton undergarments only. Take the time for hobbies and an outdoor routine (minimum of one hour) before 10 a.m. so that you can exercise and take the right amount of sunshine also.

Every woman should know about hormone replacement therapy, side effects of medicines, and various diagnostic tests and surgeries.

The moment you have any gynaecological disorder, the first thing prescribed is hormones to balance the periods. The only natural hormones are the ones that your body produces, so it is very important that before you embark on the therapy of HRT or medicines, you need to be aware about the effect they have on the cause or if they work only on the effect. Also, the emergency of your situation plays an important role because saving a life is more important than maintaining a holistic or navakarma philosophy.

Just as processed-foods and beverages companies spend a sizable chunk on advertisement and create a false desire, similarly the ease of being cured has made popping pills as routine exercise. If profit instead of cure or health is the ulterior motive, then every therapy, food, beverage, medicine, cosmetics, etc. will be questioned and made answerable.

The HRT (hormonal replacement therapy) side effects:

- blood clots
- breast cancer
- bloating

- breast swelling and tenderness
- heart diseases
- liver diseases
- nausea
- stroke
- vaginal bleeding.

The side effects of medicines prescribed should also be noted down so that you can inform your doctor if any these symptoms are found. Pregnant and breastfeeding women should never take any drugs without consulting a doctor.

After forty, the moment we start inching towards this bracket, the symptoms that get aggravated are constipation, acidity, ageing skin, pain in bones, pain in joints, spondylitis, osteoporosis, arthritis, obesity, blood pressure, heart diseases, thyroid, menopause, infertility, poor vision, mental stress, etc.

Hormone production decreases, and this causes the change. Most us are attracted towards HRT as it provides anti-ageing hormones and for curing infertility.

We want to live longer, healthier, and forever. So we have to take measures to control ageing. To take them or not is not the debate. Sometimes you might need them in an emergency situation. The global market for the human growth hormone is growing at a rapid pace and is expected to post a CAGR of 4 (22 per cent from 2015–2019). The major drivers of this market are the hormones for postmenopausal hazards. The rest of the market is for growth and thyroid hormones.

The magic of staying young is in your control. You might be taking the best diet and food supplements, but if you are emotionally drained out, then nothing external can work for you or on you. Infertility is also a major reason hormones are required. The need to have your own offspring is a natural desire for which a woman will go to any extent, but she should be made aware of the precautions and risks associated in her future life.

Facts to Know Before Going in for Surgeries Like Hysterectomy and Caesarean

Caesarean Hysterectomy—is it a medical reality or a scam?

The value of surgery is undeniable in innumerable cases. It is life-saving.

Dear readers, you might feel that I am trying to focus on why not to get the uterus removed. There can be instances that demand removal, but if the cancer risk is ruled out, then one must give a chance to reverse the symptoms that have manifested the disease. Say, a large cyst has formed over the ovary. It can press on the urinary bladder and cause discomfort. Any toxin present will also cause fever and a general debilitated feeling, depression, fear, etc. If we focus on reducing the cyst by following natural methods and if we succeed and the cyst is gone, then all the other associated symptoms will also go away. It will take time, effort, focus, willpower, and reasonable amount of patience. Any disease does not crop up suddenly, so how can we expect immediate recovery? We have all made some routine, food habits, nature of response to life's situations, which have been with us, deep-rooted just like our family's traditions, and we are accustomed to it.

A simple fact that you hear from most of the people around you is 'I lose my temper very fast'. Now if you do not take any remedial action, the continuous anger will release negative hormones. I am not questioning the value of surgery, but is it the solution that will ensure that other diseases will not manifest after surgical removal and the patient continues with the same lifestyle that causes the disease? Here I would ask the patients to be participants in their diagnosis.

It has been found that displaced hormones in the body over a period of time can manifest as diseases, like high blood pressure, thyroid, anxiety, etc.

I was reading that lakhs and lakhs of daily uterus surgeries are performed throughout the world. I am reproducing an article which mentions the grim reality.

The problems are not 'India only' problems. Unwanted hysterectomies have also been an ongoing issue in the United States. 'Each year 750, 000 hysterectomies are performed and 2,500 women die during the operation. These are not sick women but healthy women who go into the hospital and do not come out,' says Dr Herbert Goldfarb, a gynaecologist and assistant clinical professor at New York University School of Medicine in his book *No Hysterectomy Option: Your Body–Your Choice.*

So you can imagine, if we start calculating these deceptive surgeries, then the figure runs in crores or billions, and I was reading somewhere that 90 per cent are unwarranted. So if you are amongst those unwarranted ones, then you have cheated yourself on a procedure that was not required.

Menstrual syndrome at different ages will give complex varieties of symptoms. We are all living in a much more complex world which has less percentage of oxygen, chemicals have entered the food chain, waterways, environment, etc. But then most of the common diseases, like heart problems, are being managed by keeping the heart in the system because the option of removal cannot be given. Similarly, we have to take the decision along with our doctors to save the uterus. Hysterectomies are not the only panacea for all menstrual syndromes. Crucial information after surgical removal has to be shared with the patients so that they are aware of the side effects and are able to supplement themselves accurately to lead a healthy life.

Some of the symptoms that manifest after uterus removal are listed here.

- mental weakness
- endocrine system gets disturbed
- weight gain
- insomnia
- low libido
- depression.

In today's environment, we have to know the fact that the age for natural menopause is getting preponed. If hormonal imbalance is striking earlier than required, then we can choose natural menopause over surgical menopause. We should keep tabs on all the changes that we are experiencing, and if there is anything alarming, then we should definitely look at the allopathy world, which is more research based and evolved and focusses on immediate survival tactics.

Also, we are stormed with advertisements of health clinics showing hysterectomy advertisements in newspaper and various medias as if it were as simple an operation like tooth extraction. By glorifying the comfort associated with hysterectomies, they are playing with our minds, and so going under the surgeon's knife becomes the easiest option. Not very many doctors/hospitals/institutions are advertising or promoting literature or solutions to save the reproductive organs.

From the psychological/holistic angle, I also feel that the womb or uterus is the seat of our creation, where something related to our soul has done the act of creating life, babies, etc. We sometimes hear of incidents when the heart/kidney/liver transplants are done and the recipients have shown donor symptoms, like taste, habits, emotional reflexes; this proves that memories are stored in the organs also. So surgical removal cannot be without side effects, especially emotions at the subconscious level. We also know that most of our creativity and solutions come from our subconscious mind.

The operation hysterectomy should be considered as the very last form of treatment for the various conditions of reproductive organs, and the patient should have full understanding of the long-term effects of having the uterus, cervix, and/or ovaries removed.

Even Caesarean (C-section) has saved so many women and their babies, but the ease of the surgery has made this a necessity now.

Today, C-sections represent 31. 8 per cent of all births in the US annually. That's more than 1.3 million births. And that number continues to rise. In fact, in the last decade, the rate of C-sections in the US has grown by more than 50 per cent.

Natural birth is slowly being replaced by caesarean births in India. Educated and well-to-do women are going for C-section for convenience. The ease of this practice has entered the villages and economically weaker sections of the society. Unscrupulous medical practitioners are taking on the gullible rural and backward regions and raking in money.

Go to this web page to read more: http://qz.com/326402/ cesarean-births-in-india-are-skyrocketing-and-there-is-reason-to-be-very-worried/.

Visit the webpages listed below to know about the way these surgeries are being misused for financial gains:

- http://www.ndtv.com/india-news/womb-removal-andhras-big-medical-scandal-428957
- http://www.bbc.com/news/world-asia-india-19546216
- http://indianexpress.com/tag/nrhm-uterus-removal-scandal/

- http://timesofindia.indiatimes.com/city/mumbai/
  Pvt-docs-brainwash-young-women-to-go-in-for-
  hysterectomy-Survey/articleshow/50870500.com
- http://daily.bhaskar.com/news/MP-BHO-
  shocking-7-doctors-banned-for-just-an-year-over-
  uterus-removal-scandal-in-raipur-4302443-NOR.
  html
- http://www.telegraph.co.uk/women/womens-
  life/11403155/Irish-symphysiotomy-scandal-
  Doctor-used-a-hacksaw-during-labour.html
- https://www.theguardian.com/world/2006/
  mar/01/owenbowcott.mainsection.

It has been found in less-literate populations especially in the villages, womb removal surgeries are advised by unscrupulous doctors for simple abdomen pain. The naive women are convinced to undergo surgeries for a few hundred rupees so that the doctors can claim insurance from listed nursing homes. There is an instance of a twenty-year-old tribal woman who had persistent gynaecological problems, and she was advised full hysterectomy. She had already hit menopause.

'Get your uterus removed, or you will die' is the subtle message that is given to you, so this practice has to come under the lens of the authorities.

On the other hand, there is lot of research going on to do transplant of the uterus for infertility or similar issues. This is saving the uterus or giving a new lease of life to the uterus. In this method, the transplant is from a healthy donor (not living but, say, accidental death etc.).

I came across this article when I was surfing the Net. It stated that the first uterus transplant in the US had failed due to certain complications (https://www.theguardian.com/us-news/2016/mar/09/first-uterus-transplant-us-fails-lindsey-cleveland-clinic).

If transplant of a healthy uterus in an unhealthy environment can fail, then what more can be achieved by removing an unhealthy uterus (not cancerous) from a diseased person?

Removing the uterus just for swelling or pain is a violation of human rights.

So this is a multicrore- or multibillion-dollar industry, and you need to decide how much you wish to contribute to it. Also, if governments can spend money on educating girls/women on maintaining good health, then the society at large will benefit from the hand that rocks the cradle.

Mental Diet Plan

Women are known for always wanting to look slim, and most of the dieting programs are directed towards them. I would suggest mental dieting as a potent tool to life nourishment.

1. *Type of thoughts.* Avoid the company of individuals who are criticising, gossiping, creating hindrances. Nurture only those relationships that create good thoughts.
2. *Appreciation.* Avoid unappreciative friends, relatives. Life is a gift. Open yourself to the world.

3. *Peace.* Bring calmness by nurturing your children and family and by practising spirituality, meditation, and hobbies.
4. *Willpower.* Exercise control over your food habits, daily routine, and time management.
5. Look at your personal needs, wants, and desires. Worship your 'self'.

Five-Point Agenda to Look Attractive < or > Than in All Age Groups

1. *Enthusiasm.* If you are an energetic and confident person, then you automatically exude a positive image.
2. *Eyes.* They are the windows to your soul. So a twinkle in your eyes adds a lot to your charm.
3. *Smile.* It is the curve that puts everything straight and spreads the splendour of being a human being most beautifully. Having a sense of humour means you have a lot of common sense about life.
4. *Health.* Being fit and robust is more welcome than being thin and weak.
5. *Positive.* If in this moment you are positive, then your coming moments will also be positive.

Let us endeavour so to live that when we come to die even the undertaker will be sorry.

Mark Twain

Live well. Live better. Appreciate life.

Using the Nine Navakarmas for Solving Life's Problems

Life will have hurdles and problems.

The nine steps or actions are natural to the state of contentment, bliss, harmony. If you are undergoing a relationship crisis, mental trauma, financial distress, loss, failure, etc., then find yourself a place where you are not disturbed and take a deep breath and see or write how you will go about achieving balance from the current imbalance.

The first step is to unclutter your mind and to objectively apply all nine steps to your life's conditions. Remember, repetition is very important. Just meditating or exercising once can make you feel good on that particular day. Consuming nutritious food only once in a while will be of little help.

1. knowledge or gyan for mental balance
2. food or khaan for nutritional balance
3. water or pan for water balance
4. allopathy, Ayurveda, homeopathy, minerics therapy for health balance
5. exercise/yoga for body balance

6. meditation or dhyana for spiritual balance
7. work or kaam for social balance
8. charity or daan for emotional balance
9. application and assimilation of advice or saam for holistic balance

Say, you have lost your job. Use knowledge to overcome your jobless state by applying to all possible platforms—say, job portals, connecting to recruiters, e-mailing profiles to target companies, linking on social media platform. Action is the starting point.

Navakarma of Gyan

We all meet people in our lifetime who have defied the challenges life places in front of them with sheer grit and determination. I also came across one such person. I was holidaying at a place called Pachmarhi, which is a hill station around 258 kilometres from Nagpur. Near Pachmarhi, there is a mountain called Chauragarh, which is around 10 kilometres one way. This is a religious pilgrimage, and you come across people from all age groups chanting hymns and climbing the mountains. The path has some straight roads, but the rest is full of high, low, and crooked steps and pathways.

When I embarked on this journey, I had made preparations of all the snacks, juices, refreshments that I would need to carry to enjoy the journey. Huffing and puffing when I was on the trail, I was also toying with the idea of going back to the comfort of my hotel room, only to notice a frail polio-affected young girl in her teens with one hand on one knee, limping and taking quick steps on the treacherous path. Unlike me, she had no bag or any refreshment packet to fall back upon. She might have been an ordinary human being, but she had extraordinary willpower and conviction. We both were on the same destination, facing challenges of different kinds, but at that point, she was my inspiration. She might not have physical balance, but she definitely showed mental and spiritual balance.

Sometimes we tend to be a bigger obstacle to the goal rather than strive for the goal.

Navakarma of Kaam or Work

There is a masseur who visits our neighbourhood to give her services. She does not have a complete left arm, but she has mastered the art of physiotherapy and uses her feet and right arm and hand to treat patients. She is a winner. She has become a caregiver. She is facing the real world using karma or action and not succumbing to the challenge.

Navakarma for Handling Diabetes

1. Study the causes and functions of pancreas and insulin.
2. Study the foods to avoid or take.
3. Consume water for detoxification.
4. Study what modern medicine to use for immediate relief from symptoms so that harmful effects are

controlled—Ayurveda for detoxification of the pancreas, panchakarma for strengthening body fluids and metabolism, homeopathy/minercs for curing the imbalance of body salts.

5. Yoga has specific postures or *asnas* for diabetes.
6. In meditation, the manipura/solar plexus gets the most affected. The beej mantra is *ram*. Take up sound/light meditation for this specific chakra.
7. Keep yourself engaged in your profession or work.
8. Take up positive engagements, like providing services to the needy, doing charity, serving the society. Pursue your hobbies, and sharpen your skills.
9. Do all the above daily.

Navakarma for PCOS

1. Understand why PCOS happened to you.
2. Read about foods to avoid or take, and follow a strict diet plan.
3. Drink fresh water to remove accumulated toxins.
4. Modern medicine along with Ayurveda and panchakarma will strengthen your immune system. Homeopathy/minerics will treat the imbalance.
5. Yoga/exercises have to be done as a regime.
6. In meditation, the entire glandular system has to be addressed so all the beej mantras are important. You can emphasise more on the vam beej mantra as the swadhisthana or sacral chakra is blocked primarily.
7. Keep yourself occupied, and take charge of any negative thoughts and fears.

8. Engage in social work. Serve the less privileged.
9. Take charge of your body, and make this discipline a habit so that you are fit for life.

These navakarmas already exist in this world. A disciple exists in each one of us, but the guru identifies the disciple worthy of his/her teachings and not vice versa. The guru searches for the disciple who has the potential to learn and adapt the practice. The disciple is ignorant, so he cannot identify the guru. To become the right disciple for navakarma, you have to open yourself fully to receive the learning and philosophies. In holistic healing, you unite your internal spirit or energy with external spirit or energy. This is done by practice where a point comes that you become one with the external spirit. Although we are part of continuous changes internally and externally, some things—like sun, moon, life giving and taking energy, fire, water—are eternal. To enjoy eternal life, we have to know these sources. Just knowing creates a sense of well-being. Understanding leads to cleansing, and practising leads to liberation.

Glossary

panchakarma
: panchakarma *pancha (Hindi word)* means five, and *karma* means 'procedures'; an Ayurvedic practice for detoxification.

yoga nidra
: *nidra* means 'sleep'; Sleeping with awareness using Yogic meditation or mantras

rudraksha
: *rudra* signifies the Hindu deity Lord Shiva, and *aksha* means 'teardrops'; brown seed used as prayer beads by Hindus

kundali or kundli
: astrological forecast or horoscope

Mahamritunjay Jaap
: *maha* means 'great', *mrityun* means 'death', *jay* means 'victory', and *jaap* means 'recitation'. In Hindu spirituality, this recitation is done to conquer death or deathlike situations.

Google/googling
: a search engine for acquiring information on someone or something on the Internet

uterus	a hollow muscular organ (almost the size of a pear) located in the pelvic cavity of female mammals; also known as the womb
myometrium	smooth wall of the uterus
Pap test	a screening procedure for detecting precancerous or cancerous cells in the cervix
mantra	a group of words or a single word or sound which is repeated or chanted to aid concentration or meditation; sacred in nature
tantra	ancient Indian ritual to channel the divine energy from the macrocosm or godhead to microcosm
astrologer	a person who studies astrology, which is the study of the motions and relative positions of the planets, sun, and moon interpreted in terms of human characteristics and activities
benign	not malignant, not cancerous
malignant	cancerous
atypia	a irregular or nonstandard structural abnormality in a cell
hyperprogestationalised	all maternal systems subjected to increasing levels of circulating progesterone

stromal cellls | stromal cells that support the function of the parenchymal cells of that organ (fibroblasts and pericytes are amongst the most common types of stromal cells)

decidualisation | may be used to describe any change due to progesterone

iatrogenic | induced inadvertently by a physician or surgeon or by medical treatment or diagnostic procedures

About the Author

Shreya Nath, born in India, is currently residing at Nagpur, Maharashtra. She is a science graduate from Delhi University with an MBA in marketing and systems. She is a regular practitioner of chakra meditation and is involved in various social causes. She is an entrepreneur and is the CEO/founder of *Headstart* (www.headstartindia.in), an executive search firm established in 1999.